Strategic Thinking

A Guide to Identifying and Solving Problems

BY ROGER KAUFMAN

Illustrations by Gary Carroll

W9-CCE-169

ASTD
AMERICAN SOCIETY FOR TRAINING AND DEVELOPMENT

Copublished by the American Society for Training and Development and the International Society for Performance Improvement

Ordering information: Books published by ASTD can be ordered by calling 703/683-8100; to order books published by ISPI, call 202/408-7969.

Library of Congress Catalog Card Number: 96-084117

ISBN:1-56286-051-8

CONTENTS

i

PREFACE

The world always seems to be turning upside down. Nothing stands still, nothing seems predictable anymore. What was safe, sure, and secure yesterday doesn't work today. Increasingly what we deliver, do, and use seems out of focus. So, how do we deal with tomorrow? Do we do more of the same but with increased energy and dedication? Do we look over into other people's patches, play follow-the-leader, and copy whatever they seem to be doing that seems to work?

As things change, it becomes increasingly important to think strategically, keeping two factors in mind: problem solving and creating the future. We must build a new tomorrow. Because the world is unpredictable and full of surprise, we have to identify and resolve problems. And, at the same time, we have to seek new opportunities. We must create the future we want.

Why both? If we wait for problems to appear, we are always reacting, trying to fix whatever seems to be broken. If we also look ahead—anticipate and create a new future and shift our thinking about organizations, people, and resources before problems occur—we will move ahead of everyone else. Handling problems and seeking new opportunities are keys to a successful future. This book is about both.

Strategic Thinking: A Guide to Identifying and Solving Problems might, without careful examination, seem to be suggesting the same old things you've heard before, especially since this book is built in part on previous works, including *Identifying and Solving Problems*. (And some might wonder why it has taken me so long to get it right.) Much of the basics remain unchanged, such as means and ends, setting measurable objectives, needs and needs assessment, and the Organizational Elements Model. These basics are solid and proven. The basics of how to shift from quick fixes and solutions-in-search-of-problems to a practical and pragmatic system approach all stand as tried and true methods. While the methods remain unchanged, *Strategic Thinking* has been substantially modified and clarified based on years of use and feedback.

Look for additional concepts, tools, and considerations that bring this problem solving process to life and guide you to define and achieve success. Also included are the following: six critical success factors; Mega-, Macro-, and Micro-level thinking, planning, and doing based on who is to be the primary client and beneficiary of what gets done and delivered; deriving and using an Ideal Vision for guiding all that you plan, do, and deliver; and quality management is defined and integrated with this approach to strategic thinking and identifying and solving problems.

This book is basic and straightforward. It provides both the basics for defining and achieving success and a toolkit that offers some practical guidance.

The details for each of the tools and techniques are available elsewhere—this is a guide, not a handbook. Useful resources are noted in the back by numbers in the text. Everything you have to have to shift your paradigms is here. It will allow you to change, sensibly and not blindly, from the old and comfortable ways that don't serve you well anymore, to new ones that are responsible, responsive, pragmatic, and practical. This book will help you take control of the future and help shape it instead of always asking, "What happened?" and "How do we fix our problems?" The future is yours to create and enjoy.

ACKNOWLEDGMENTS

What is here has been developed over many years as others have attempted to educate me. Among those who have tried their best (but don't own any of the flaws in me, my work, or this book) include graduate students at Florida State University and the United States International University, as well as other academic institutions who have invited me to work with them; faculty and learners at other postsecondary institutions; professionals who have to identify and solve problems at private and public sector organizations around the world who have either used my work and/or me; and friends, relatives, and acquaintances who have helped make this work better than it would have been.

I appreciate publishing this with the two strongest professional organizations in Performance Improvement in the world, the American Society for Training and Development and the International Society for Performance Improvement. Both organizations, like me, are committed to helping you be successful.

The Florida State University and the Learning Systems Institute have provided me the environment in which to think, apply, and learn. My colleagues at the Center for Needs Assessment and Planning work with me daily to think issues through and to apply what appears here to our work: Phil Grise, Kathi Watters, Ryan Watkins, Don Triner, and Leon Sims work on me all of the time. The staff and students also do their best to keep me realistic. Helpful suggestions were provided by Ken Modesitt of the University of Michigan–Dearborn and by Paul MacGillis of the Florida Department of Labor. Jean Van Dyke restrained herself during endless runs through the word processor. My partner, Jan Kaufman, always works with me in life and delivers continuous encouragement and the surroundings that it takes to think and write. Special thanks are due Gary Carroll for creating the graphics—he applied his skills by working through the concept.

Many of the concepts and tools presented here are used with the permission of several publishers who have had confidence in my work. I would like to thank Technomic Publishing, Sage Publications, and Corwin Press.

But the most thanks go to you, the reader. Without you, and your sensible and pragmatic application of this and earlier works, I would not be offering this book. I look forward to working with you again.

Roger Kaufman
Tallahassee, Florida
March 1996

REFERENCES AND RELATED READINGS

A note to the Reader: This book is divided into two parts, What and How. In the first part, the tools and exercises that might be useful to you are noted with a sign denoting the toolkit section, where you can find help.

Part 1: The "Whats" of Strategic Thinking and Planning

One

Getting the Right Focus: Paradigms, Reality, and Success

Sometimes the world does seem to be turned upside down.

Things we could count on yesterday aren't true today.

- Japan makes cheap junk, and copies at that.
- My neighborhood is safe.
- Gasoline is 29 cents a gallon.
- High school graduates can read and write.
- The air and water are clean and will stay that way.
- Asia is backward.

Most things we used to believe don't apply any more—

There is much more to read about this. See the following references: 2, 3, 4, 5, 6, 7, 8, 10, 11, 12, 13, 14, 15, 16, 18, 19, 21, 24, 32, 33, 34, 35, 38, 39, 41, 42, 43, 44, 45, 46, 47, 48, 49, 50, 51, 53, 54.

- working harder will make you successful;
- we can always replace a worker with a cheaper one;
- get a bachelor's degree and get a good job;
- close supervision pays;
- a day's work for a day's pay;
- some work is only for men, and some only for women;
- management tells, workers do;
- you have to fight workers (or management) for everything you get;
- workers don't have useful ideas;
- make sure we have all the numbers before making a decision;
- see what the competition is doing and do it too;
- the cheaper you make something, the better;
- let the buyer beware;
- sell, sell, sell;
- we can take our time and be linear in our planning and work.

What worked yesterday might not work today or tomorrow.

Things seem out of focus!

Our old ways of viewing and interacting with our world—our guides, our rules, regulations, and boundaries—have changed. Our PARADIGMS have shifted.

Thomas Kuhn and Joel Barker have a lot to say on this, and so does Peter Drucker.

Some of us prefer "frame of reference" to PARADIGM.

PARADIGMS—we all have them.

1 + 1 = 2
1 + 1 = 11
1 + 1 = 2 or 11
1 + 1 = yes and yes

These are different PARADIGMS for (1+1). The last one is "computerese."

PARADIGMS are the boundaries and ground rules we use to filter reality.

PARADIGMS allow us to understand our world, and to deal with it. (2, 3, 4, 35, 36, 38, 39, 40, 41)

New PARADIGMS will help us think strategically.

When you want to know more, these numbers are keyed to the references in the back.

PARADIGMS are useful. We employ them constantly.

We have PARADIGMS for
- business,
- competition,
- family,
- friends,
- politics,
- life,
- death.

And books that go on and on after making a point!

Sometimes our old PARADIGMS will get us into trouble. They might cause us to see new things as threats, and not as the opportunities they might be. For example, xerography, computers, quartz movement watches, quality management/continuous improvement, and MEGA planning, to name only a few paradigm shifts others did not adopt and exploit early in their appearance.(1) Keeping and using our current PARADIGMS will keep us in our comfort zones—but is it only comfort we are after?

New PARADIGMS—expanded or using different boundaries and ground rules—will help us shape new success. Instead of trying to use old approaches, tools, and understandings, we will create new—and better—realities. Find the "right" focus.

This book provides some new PARADIGMS (and tools) for
- identifying problems;
- identifying opportunities;
- resolving problems;
- defining and achieving success;
- systematic thinking and planning;
- finding synergies among tools and approaches;
- thinking strategically;
- thinking in wholes and not in parts;
- adding value;
- creating the future.

But, often new PARADIGMS get you out of your comfort zones.
Beware—when out of your comfort zones, you can (20)
- get defensive,
- get angry,
- get abusive,
- or just not get the message.

When any of this material shifts you to discomfort, take a deep breath, open up, and ask yourself, "Besides being uncomfortable, is my current way really successful, or do I just know how to operate this way?"

Not adopting (or adapting) a new and useful paradigm might be the most dangerous decision you can make. (2, 3, 4)

And finding opportunities as well. (11, 19)

So important is this PARADIGM possibility that it is the first—and most basic—Critical Success Factor for thinking strategically and for identifying and resolving important problems.

Critical Success Factor #1

Move out of your comfort zones—today's PARADIGMS—and use new, wider boundaries for thinking, planning, doing, and continuous improvement/evaluating.

You'll be getting 6 Critical Success Factors before the end of this book. (10, 11)

So what was this chapter about?

1. Getting the right focus. What we concentrate on doing and delivering is vital for strategic success.

2. PARADIGMS—the boundaries and ground rules we use to understand and deal with our world—should be selected and used based on reality, not just comfort.

3. Selecting useful (and often new) PARADIGMS will help us think and act strategically.

4. Be ready and willing to shift your PARADIGMS. Select PARADIGMS that are larger and more inclusive when there has been a paradigm shift, and there have been many paradigm shifts in our world. And more are on the way!

Let's go to some of the other factors in being successful
at identifying and solving problems.

Two

Understanding Ends and Means: Three Levels of Results and the Organizational Elements Model

NEEDS AND WANTS—AN IMPORTANT DIFFERENCE

Sometimes people want us to "buy" their solution before we really know what the problem is. That's what those headlines on the previous page are all about. We say we "need" luxuries, products, money, programs, services—all kinds of things we don't currently have. But, do we believe that these things will possibly fulfill NEEDS or do we think they are NEEDS? That's more than just an idle question.

We can save money, time, human resources, and frustration if we can stop jumping into solutions before we are sure what our problem really is.

NEEDS and wants are not the same. Neither are problems and solutions the same! (34, 35, 36, 38, 39)

Picture this scene.

Just why do you "need" (or desire or require) a car, and/or a new car, and/or a new Jaguar convertible car? And why, in particular, use the word "need" in the statement? Maybe someone is trying to "sell" something as a necessity or an imperative when it really isn't! Maybe a new Jaguar is just one of several alternatives (or options) for meeting the real NEED. But saying "I need" cuts out even the recognition of other possible solutions—it screams for a single solution, or means, without first defining the problem.

It will help to divide this concept into two parts, ENDS and MEANS, and see how it works for our car example.

MEANS	ENDS
Feet Bicycle 4-wheel drive Motorcycle Minivan Economy car	Transportation for work and pleasure
Jaguar Mercedes Yacht Private plane	Status

It is obvious that most of the time when we use the word NEED (as a verb), we jump right over other possible MEANS (or options) and lock ourselves in to a solution that might not be the best one to reach the desired END.

SOLUTION A   **SOLUTION B**   **SOLUTION C**

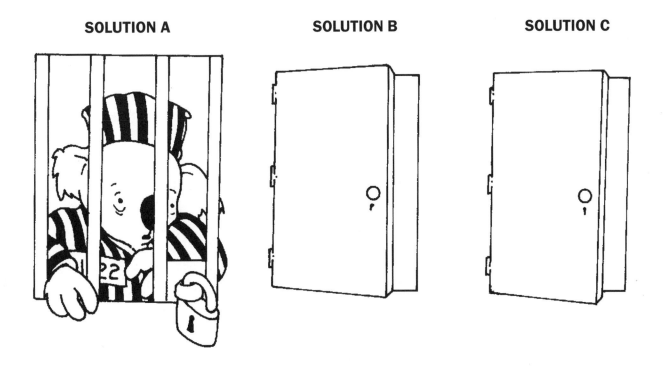

This brings us to our Critical Success Factor #2.

Define NEED as a gap in results—between current and desired results—not as insufficient levels of resources, MEANS, or how-to-do-its.

Keep in mind Critical Success Factor #1, move out of your comfort zones—today's PARADIGMS—and use new, wider boundaries for thinking, planning, doing, and continuous improvement/evaluating.

Critical Success Factor #2 will help us keep ENDS and MEANS related—let's see.

We often jump to premature solutions and get over our heads in our problems. When we use NEED to prescribe, we reduce a person's choice for the freedom to define their own problems. When we reduce people's choices, we get negative empowerment.

We should select our MEANS based on the ENDS we wish to achieve.

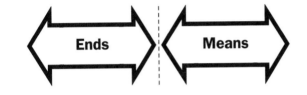

This confusion is found everywhere. For example, these opinions really are solutions, in search of a problem.

- No subsidies for transportation
- Ban cars
- Pro-life
- Pro-choice
- Private education
- Accountability
- Raise taxes
- Lower taxes
- Only public education
- Work harder!
- More jobs
- More leisure
- Build more prisons
- Move slowly and deliberately
- If it ain't broke, don't fix it
- Benchmarking
- Reengineering

Although well-intentioned, many solutions are not linked to important ENDS. When MEANS and ENDS are not linked sensibly, we often fail—even with the best of intentions! So, often we have solutions in search of problems!

Let's not confuse MEANS and ENDS!

Because that's a lot of work to go nowhere.

Let's use the same words to mean the same things! Here are some definitions.

END: A result, OUTCOME, OUTPUT, or PRODUCT.

MEANS: The tools, methods, techniques, resources, or PROCESS used to achieve an END.

NEED: The gap between current results (or ENDS) and desired results (or ENDS). Notice that NEED as used in Strategic Thinking and Planning is a noun, not a verb; it is also not used in the sense of a verb.

PROBLEM: A NEED selected for closure; a gap to be closed.

Let's see how these definitions can work for us. The customers (81 percent) of a bank say, "We 'need' longer banking hours." The vice-presidents (77 percent) say, "We 'need' shorter banking hours." Tellers (67 percent) say, "We 'need' higher pay."

Look like a conflict? Maybe not; perhaps each group has confused MEANS and ENDS and jumped right to solutions (higher pay, shorter hours, longer hours) without defining the NEED as a gap between current results (or ENDS) and desired results.

Let's see what each group is saying in terms of MEANS and ENDS.

MEANS	ENDS
Customers: longer banking hours	?
Vice-Presidents: shorter banking hours	?
Tellers: more money	?

No ENDS or results are stated! We may only infer them. Without knowing the results we want, how can we sensibly choose among possible MEANS?

Before rushing into any solution (even if someone calls it a NEED), we first should define and justify the ENDS to be accomplished. It really makes more sense to decide how to do something after we know what we are to accomplish.

ENDS

↗   ↑   ↖

means   means   means

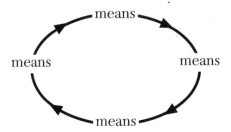

Try to sort some of the "hot" issues in contemporary living into MEANS and ENDS.

ISSUES	MEANS	ENDS
Welfare		
Abortion		
Open-choice education		
Jobs		
Decreased government spending		
Preserving the environment		
Downsizing		

Do all these turn out to be solutions in search of problems? Will MEANS produce desired ENDS? Do proposers of MEANS link their solutions to desired results—or do they just hope that they will be useful?

If you're not part of the solution, you're part of the problem.

The issues listed above all are MEANS!

Whoa! Before rushing into a solution, let's begin by defining terms. Perhaps we do not know the real problem!

We can argue almost forever about MEANS—

- If we don't know what we want to accomplish or why we want it accomplished,
- If we don't define the appropriate ENDS, or OUTCOMES,
- If we confuse NEEDS and wants, and ENDS and MEANS.

And when we refer to a means we want as a "NEED," we do jump prematurely to a solution. That can bring big trouble!

> "A poorly defined problem may have an infinite number of solutions."

Whoever said that must have worked in my office.

To properly relate ENDS and MEANS, remember to define a NEED as a gap in results, not a gap in processes, tools, or resources.

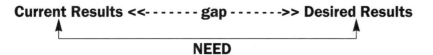

Current Results <<- - - - - - - gap - - - - - - ->> Desired Results

NEED

MEANS are ways and resources to meet the NEED—to close the gaps between "What-is-results" and "What-should-be-results."

NEEDS ASSESSMENTS
- identify NEEDS (as gaps in results),
- prioritize the NEEDS,
- select the most important NEEDS for elimination or reduction.

NEEDS ASSESSMENTS should not focus on means (such as training) or resources (such as money or people). MEANS and resources should be chosen only after identifying and selecting the NEEDS.

Toolkit
I

By defining NEEDS as gaps in results you can be more successful.
NEEDS versus wants, MEANS and ENDS—carefully relating these will make you

```
effective
and
efficient
and
humane.
```

Remember to first define (and justify) the ENDS before choosing the MEANS.

Because NEEDS focus on ENDS, not MEANS, this bring us to our Critical Success Factor #3.

Differentiate between ENDS and MEANS—focus on what before selecting how.

Okay, that's three out of six.

Remember the first two Critical Success Factors.
#1: Move out of your comfort zones—today's PARADIGMS—and use new, wider boundaries for thinking, planning, doing, and continuous improvement/evaluating.
#2: Define NEED as a gap in results—between current and desired results—not as insufficient levels of resources, MEANS, or how-to-do-its.

Shall we try differentiating between ENDS and MEANS? Sort the following into MEANS and ENDS.

Learning problem solving
Getting a job
Having positive self-esteem
Joining a class action law suit
Downsizing
Moving to Fiji
Graduating from college
Survival
Loving
Banning tree cutting
Reengineering

MEANS	ENDS

	MEANS	ENDS
Learning problem solving	√	
Getting a job	√	?
Having positive self-esteem	?	?
Joining a class action law suit	√	?
Downsizing	√	?
Moving to Fiji	√	?
Graduating from college	√	?
Survival		√
Loving	?	?
Banning tree cutting	√	?
Reengineering	√	

Why all those question marks?

You are right! Sometimes something is a building block to a larger result and/or payoff and sometimes it may also be a final END.

Some of us want to love so that we will be loved in return, and will feel secure and accepted. We might want to get a job to make money, buy a car, or graduate from college, or we might want to stop cutting down trees to assure we have a livable environment so that nothing unintentionally goes extinct.

Each milestone result along the way to a large END can be perceived as an END in itself, or as a building block to a larger or more distant END. But what is most important to the success of any venture is to make sure that there is a clear, defined, and justified result we are aiming for—an END to be achieved. Actually, in the previous list, "survive" is probably the only basic OUTCOME; the others really relate most to quality of survival. We must make certain that there is a well-defined distinction and relationship between ENDS and MEANS!

Each time you plan do something, consider what you want to achieve both now and later as a result of this achievement.

Looks like we are building up to a hierarchy of results.

Right! That is exactly where we are headed.

But to keep MEANS and ENDS in perspective, ask yourself, "If I do or accomplish this, what will be the result?"

If it already is an END, you will know it. If not, this approach will help keep you focused on results.

Keep asking yourself this question until you have identified the END. You then will have shifted focus from MEANS to ENDS, from solutions to problems, from how to what.

There are several kinds of results. Some results are desired by an organization or an individual and some are societal in nature.

You mean that what some people want to achieve is not necessarily what organizations want to achieve?

Sometimes, however, they are the same.

Let's now turn to the ORGANIZATIONAL ELEMENTS MODEL (OEM) that allows us to relate everything we use, do, produce, and deliver. (33, 34, 35, 36, 37, 39, 41)

Some results, or ENDS, are outside of (external to) our organization—they exist in society. And, some results are within an organization.

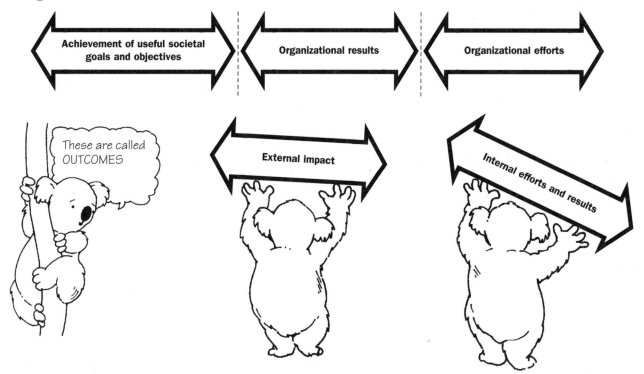

If you like, we could substitute "individual" for "organizational" in this figure.

Personal or organizational results, to be more effective, should be directly related to achievement of societal results—results that are useful in and for today and tomorrow's society.

Organizations are MEANS to societal ENDS.

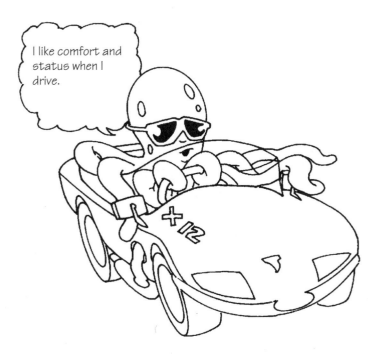

In order to differentiate between various kinds of MEANS and ENDS, we can relate them.

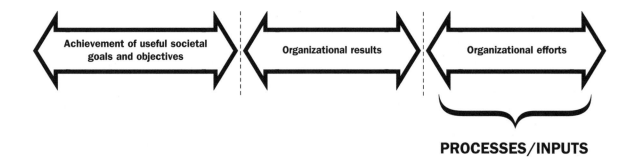

What an organization has available for its efforts is called INPUTS such as funds, people, buildings, equipment. PROCESSES are "how-to-do-its" for using the INPUTS. Both INPUTS and PROCESSES make up "organizational efforts."

Organizational efforts bring results.

The first type of result is PRODUCTS, the en route accomplishments that will be the building blocks for the second type of result, OUTPUTS.

OUTPUTS are the "organizational results" that may be delivered to society—outside the organization.

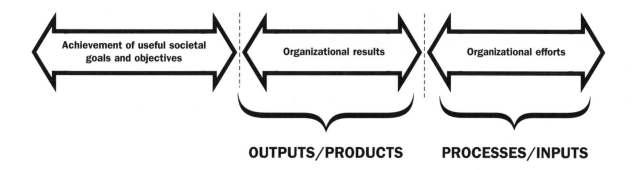

Organizational efforts yield organizational results, and organizational results have impact in and for society. The societal goals and objectives and consequences are called OUTCOMES.

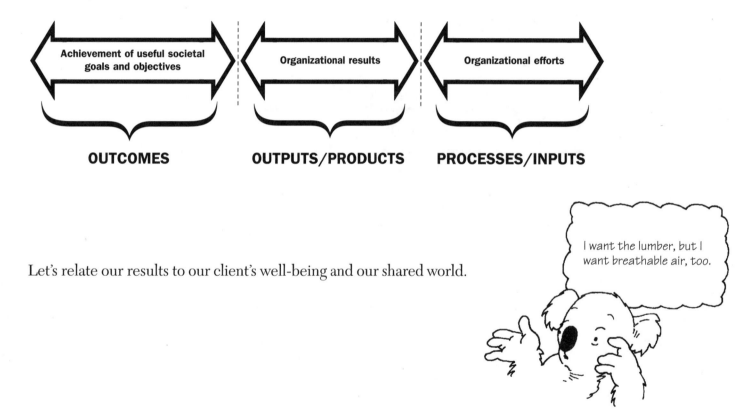

Let's relate our results to our client's well-being and our shared world.

I want the lumber, but I want breathable air, too.

There are three levels of results. Each level focuses on a different primary client and beneficiary of what gets delivered. When the primary client and beneficiary is society—including our organization's external clients—we are thinking, planning, and problem solving at the MEGA level.

MEGA Level

Primary Client	Planning Level	Type of Result
Society and clients (now and in the future)	MEGA	OUTCOMES

Is all this really necessary?

Only if you want to be successful!

The **MEGA** level is basic to all we use, do, produce, and deliver. If we don't include the **MEGA** level in our thinking and problem solving (and opportunity-finding) we might make our customers temporarily happy, but not serve them well after delivery.

Another level of results is the organizational one—where the primary client and beneficiary is the organization itself. Where the primary client and beneficiary of what is planned and delivered is the organization itself, the focus and the plan is at the MACRO level.

MACRO Level

Primary Client	Planning Level	Type of Result
Society and clients (now and in the future)	MEGA	OUTCOMES
The organization	MACRO	OUTPUTS

An example is a delivered car and/or a college graduate.

I'm a MACRO person—got to make a profit.

I'm your conscience—you also have to contribute to our shared world.

When the primary client and beneficiary is an individual (or small group), your planning and delivery is at the MICRO level. In fact, most of our efforts and attention are at the MICRO level. Our PRODUCTS are the building blocks of what we deliver to our clients—our OUTPUTS.

The payoffs from what we deliver are focused at the MEGA level.

MICRO Level

Primary Client	Planning Level	Type of Result
Society and external clients (now and in the future)	MEGA	OUTCOMES
The organization	MACRO	OUTPUTS
(Individuals or small groups)	MICRO	PRODUCTS

MICRO-level results could include
- competent assemblers with no rejects,
- trainees who can correctly refer calls,
- tellers who make no entry errors,
- first grade teachers whose learners all read at or above grade level.

I think you get the idea.

Organizations, including what they use (INPUTS), do (PROCESSES), produce (PRODUCTS), and deliver (OUTPUTS), all have to make a contribution to clients and our shared world (OUTCOMES).

All of the elements form a results chain, where each element is contributing to a common result and payoff.

Results chains:

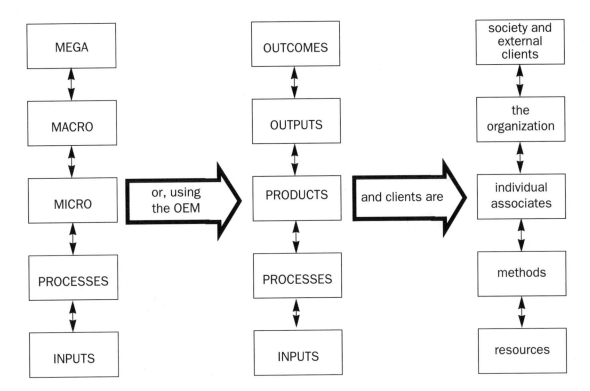

So, this brings us to Critical Success Factor #4.

Use and relate all three levels of planning and results—MEGA/OUTCOMES, MACRO/OUTPUTS, MICRO/PRODUCTS.

Doing this will give us front-end alignment.

Reminder,

#1: Move out of your comfort zones—today's PARADIGMS—and use new, wider boundaries for thinking, planning, doing, and continuous improvement/evaluating.

#2: Define NEED as a gap in results—between current and desired results—not as insufficient levels of resources, MEANS, or how-to-do-its.

#3: Differentiate between ENDS and MEANS—focus on what before selecting how.

Critical Success Factor #4 will help keep ENDS and MEANS related, and align organizational efforts, organizational results as they together achieve shared and useful societal goals and objectives—positive societal impact.

The attention to **MEGA**-level results (and payoffs) provides a plus factor to the value you (and your organization) contribute to our world.

And to your client's success as well.

When you add MEGA to your strategic planning it becomes Strategic Planning Plus.

MEGA-level planning is not only ethical, it is also very practical. Using it will add value to what you use, do, produce, and deliver.

Toolkit II

Let's see how to put this to work in Problem Solving and Strategic Thinking and Planning.

Okay, we just covered a lot of material.

- MEANS and ENDS are related, but not the same;
- NEEDS are best defined as gaps between current and desired results, not as "code" for a MEANS one really (or really, really) wants;
- When we use NEED as a verb, we usually shunt ourselves directly into MEANS (solutions)—and thus we might spend our time developing solutions to no known problem.
- There are 3 levels of results.
  - Societal, called OUTCOMES or results at the MEGA level,
  - Organizational, called OUTPUTS or results at the MACRO level,
  - Individual, or small group, called PRODUCTS or results at the MICRO level.
- Organizational efforts—INPUTS and PROCESSES—are useful only if they deliver results.
- What organizations use, do, produce, and deliver are practical only if they deliver external (MEGA-level) results and payoffs.
- The Organizational Elements Model (OEM) provides five elements that identify what every organization uses, does, produces, delivers, and the usefulness to external clients and society.

- The OEM is composed of
  - INPUTS (resources, ingredients),
  - PROCESSES (methods, means, procedures, activities),
  - PRODUCTS (building-block results),
  - OUTPUTS (what is delivered outside the organization),
  - OUTCOMES (impact and payoff for clients and society).
- Planning, what is produced and delivered, also has three levels.
  - MEGA (OUTCOMES) are societal results.
  - MACRO (OUTPUTS) are organizational contributions.
  - MICRO (PRODUCTS) are building-block results.
- The primary clients and beneficiaries differ.
  - MEGA (OUTCOMES)—society
  - MACRO (OUTPUTS)—organization
  - MICRO (PRODUCTS)—individuals
- The results of any organization should be linked, and all should have MEGA-level payoffs.

Three

Visions, Missions, and Organizational Contributions

Adding the **MEGA** level to your thinking, planning, and doing allows for practical dreaming. (35) It is very practical (and safe) to start with an **IDEAL VISION**, the kind of world we want for tomorrow's child. (35, 47, 51)

If it is ideal, it focuses only on the society in which your (and everyone else's) organization must contribute to stay viable.

Like Martin Luther King, Jr., and Walt Disney—they had dreams!

Here is an example of a minimal (most basic) IDEAL VISION:

There will be no losses of life or elimination or reduction of levels of well-being, survival, self-sufficiency, quality of life, livelihood, or loss of property from any source including but not limited to the following:

- war and/or riot,
- unintended human-caused changes to the environment, including permanent destruction of the environment and/or rendering it nonrenewable,
- murder, rape, or crimes of violence, robbery, or destruction of property,
- substance abuse,
- disease or disability,

- pollution,
- starvation and/or malnutrition,
- child abuse,
- partner/spouse abuse,
- accidents, including transportation, home, and business/workplace,
- discrimination based on irrelevant variables including color, race, creed, sex, religion, national origin, location.

Poverty will not exist, and every person will earn at least as much as it costs to live (unless they are progressing toward being self-sufficient and self-reliant). No adult will be under the care, custody, or control of another person, agency, or substance. All adult citizens will be self-sufficient and self-reliant as minimally indicated by their consumption being equal to or less than their production.

Key enablers (the most likely vehicles to achieve the minimal IDEAL VISION):

Any and all organizations—governmental, private sector/for-profit, public service/not-for-profit, educational—will contribute to the achievement and maintenance of this minimal IDEAL VISION and will be funded and continued to the extent that it meets its objectives and the minimum IDEAL VISION is accomplished and maintained.

People will be responsible for what they use, do, and contribute, and thus will not contribute to the reduction of any of the results identified in this minimal IDEAL VISION.

If our organization is the solution, what's the problem? Doing good and making money are not mutually exclusive!

Get real, world! This is nothing but pie-in-the-sky! This will never get accepted!

IDEAL VISIONS are very similar for all organizations!

And "mutual world" means international.

But if we don't head there, what do we have in mind?

Toolkit
III

An IDEAL VISION is Ideal! We might not get there in our lifetime, or our children's, but it serves as a guiding star toward which we all may navigate, make our unique contributions, and evaluate our continuous improvement and progress.

Our organizations all must contribute to moving ever closer to the IDEAL VISION.

Some planners prefer to include some more philosophical concepts in their IDEAL VISION. Doing so might help achieve more comfort.

Each of us is not solely responsible for achieving the IDEAL VISION— we form a partnership to get there. We select the part of the IDEAL VISION we commit to deliver.

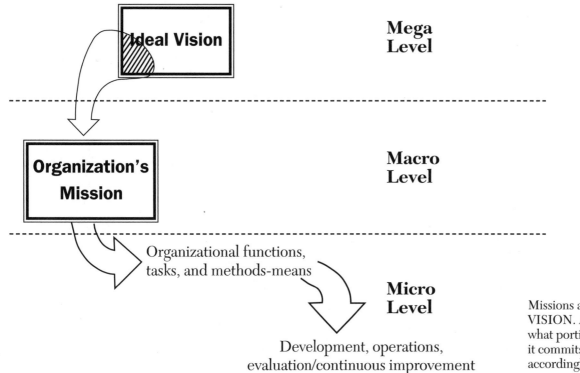

Ideal Vision

Mega Level

Organization's Mission

Macro Level

Organizational functions, tasks, and methods-means

Micro Level

Development, operations, evaluation/continuous improvement

Missions are from the IDEAL VISION. An organization will select what portion of the IDEAL VISION it commits to addressing and will act accordingly.

Let's see, the IDEAL VISION is MEGA-level results.

I can see some ways to find opportunities. Parts of the IDEAL VISION could be niches. And we can also spot redundancy and synergies as well!

The mission objective is the MACRO level of results.

Ideal Vision

Mega Level

Organization's Mission

Macro Level

Organizational functions, tasks, and methods-means

Micro Level

Development, operations, evaluation/continuous improvement

Missions are from the IDEAL VISION. An organization will select what portion of the IDEAL VISION it commits to addressing and will act accordingly.

Rummler & Brache talk about this Macro level. (50)

When we start with an IDEAL VISION and roll down from there to define our ENDS and MEANS—the organizational results and efforts—we
- link ENDS and MEANS,
- use the three levels of results,
- sensibly identify NEEDS—gaps in results—so we can get from where we are to achieving our mission, and move continuously toward our IDEAL VISION.

This approach keeps us from premature selection of means.

Hmm, if we don't define our IDEAL VISION, how do we know in which direction to take our first step? Or how to track our progress?

This really is practical—I can now justify where we are headed, and what parts of it my organization commits to deliver.

So useful is starting with an IDEAL VISION, it is our Critical Success Factor #5.

Use an **IDEAL VISION** (what kind of world, in measurable terms, we want for tomorrow's child) as the underlying basis for your thinking, planning, doing, and continuous improvement.

> And don't pay much attention to all those nay-sayers and whiners. They just are out of their comfort zones and afraid they will have to give up their old PARADIGMS.

> But be patient and listen. Make sure you hear the useful things they might suggest.

> The IDEAL VISION is about our world, not just about our organization.

Reminder, the other Critical Success Factors are

#1: Move out of your comfort zones—today's PARADIGMS—and use new, wider boundaries for thinking, planning, doing, and continuous improvement/evaluating.

#2: Define NEED as a gap in results—between current and desired results—not as insufficient levels of resources, MEANS, or how-to-do-its.

#3: Differentiate between ENDS and MEANS—focus on what before selecting how.

#4: Use and relate all three levels of planning and results—MEGA/OUTCOMES, MACRO/OUTPUTS, MICRO/PRODUCTS.

Let's stop for a moment and think about where we have been up to this point. First, we shared that the world has changed, and will continue to do so. Our old PARADIGMS and tools won't serve us well as the ground rules shift. New PARADIGMS, though sometimes uncomfortable, will have to be accepted. Second, we have to distinguish between ENDS and MEANS, between what and how. Third, it is realistic to identify and link three levels of results—MEGA/OUTCOMES, MACRO/OUTPUTS, MICRO/PRODUCTS in order to form a results chain. Fourth, the societal payoffs (MEGA-level consequences) assure us that what we use, do, produce, and deliver not only satisfy the clients, but also serve them well. An IDEAL VISION provides an ethical and practical front-end alignment.

Let's now apply all of this to Identifying and Solving Problems.

Back to basics again. Back to the differences and relationships between ENDS and MEANS.
In order to differentiate between various kinds of MEANS and ENDS, we may relate them to one another this way.

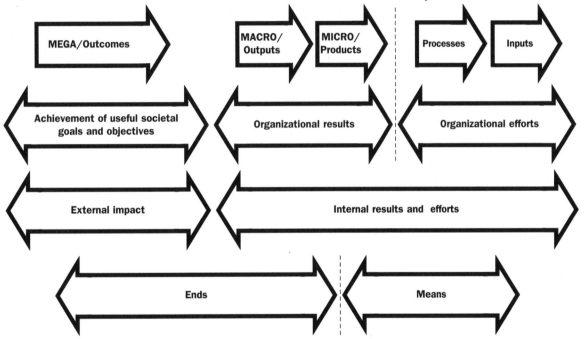

All the things we work with, use, and produce are internal, and they yield results that are visible in the short run.
And they all have impact—consequences in society—that will be seen in the long run.

These five organizational elements, when related to one another, are called the Organizational Elements Model (OEM). Its use—as we saw in Chapter Two—will allow you to relate MEANS and ENDS, and organizational (or personal) resources, efforts, and results with success in life, results at the MEGA level, all related to our IDEAL VISION.

The OEM is a guide, or template. Use it for managing for successful results and payoffs by assuring that all three levels of results link—that what you use, do, produce, and deliver is useful to everyone, and that the results bring added value to the client and to society.

Because others around us are not always precise about the words they use, here are some useful definitions.

INPUTS are the ingredients and raw materials we have to work with—those people and things with which we start. They include our existing goals and objectives.

PROCESSES are the ways in which we use, orchestrate, transform, and manage our INPUT—our how-to-do-its and methods.

PRODUCTS are the en route results we get on the way to organizational and societal results. They are "building blocks" for larger results. These are MICRO-level contributions.

OUTPUTS are the total results of the organization or individual—that which is delivered or deliverable to society. These are called MACRO-level results.

OUTCOMES are the results—and payoffs—of all the organization's efforts (INPUTS and PROCESSES) as we transform them into organizational results—PRODUCTS, and OUTPUTS. These are external to the individual or organization, and are MEGA-level contributions and payoffs.

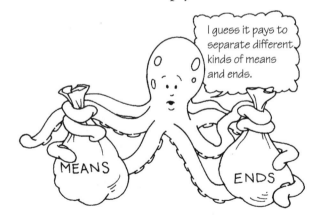

I guess it pays to separate different kinds of means and ends.

Let's look at some examples of each.

Organization

MEGA/ OUTCOMES	MACRO/ OUTPUTS	MICRO/ PRODUCTS	PROCESSES	INPUTS
• self-sufficient and contributing people • reduced or eliminated illness due to air pollution • reduced or eliminated fatalities • positive quality of life • fewer/no welfare recipients • continued profit • stockholder vote of confidence • money for continuation • zero crime • zero homelessness • client's success	• assembled automobiles • yearly auto production • automobiles sold • system delivered • production line	• tire • fender • divisional quota met • completed training manuals • trained workers • patient discharged • worker agreement • course completed • operation completed	• organization development • management techniques • manufacturing techniques • training • quality assurance • reengineering • curriculum • quality improvement programs • doing • learning • developing • examining patient • strategic planning • strategic thinking	• money • people • equipment • facilities • goals • time • resources • needs • problems (currently existing) • values • laws • regulations • history

Individual

MEGA/ OUTCOMES	MACRO/ OUTPUTS	MICRO/ PRODUCTS	PROCESSES	INPUTS
• expenses less than income • positive future • freedom from fear • financial independence • no disabling illness	• obtain first career position • marriage to loved one • good physical health • graduation from college • discharge from hospital • maintainance of desired weight	• monthly paycheck • mastery of word processing • purchase of car • clean house • dinner party held	• critical thinking • intuition • guilt • depression • task orientation • valuing • problem solving • defense mechanism • going through psychotherapy • working • planning • investing • dreaming	• money • personality • mental & physical characteristics • resources • needs • goals • desires • problems (currently existing) • values • laws • memories

The OEM is not linear or "lock-step."

When used correctly it is, in fact, very dynamic and flexible.

Usually, an INPUT leads to a PROCESS. Many times a PROCESS becomes a part of another PROCESS, such as this flow from INPUTS to two consecutive PROCESSES.

MEGA/OUTCOMES	MACRO/OUTPUTS	MICRO/PRODUCTS	PROCESSES	INPUTS
			Developing training program ②◄	Money ①
		Training program validated ④◄	Trying out training program ③	

Following these numbers shows that this is not a linear process.

Sometimes a PRODUCT may become an INPUT to be used in another PROCESS.

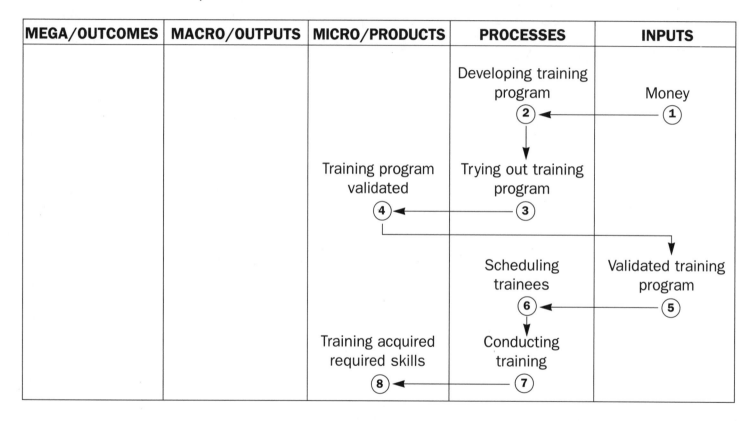

MEGA/OUTCOMES	MACRO/OUTPUTS	MICRO/PRODUCTS	PROCESSES	INPUTS
			Developing training program ② ◄─── ①	Money ①
		Training program validated ④ ◄───	Trying out training program ③	
			Scheduling trainees ⑥ ◄───	Validated training program ⑤
		Training acquired required skills ⑧ ◄───	Conducting training ⑦	

The OEM relates and interrelates
- MEANS and ENDS,
- organizational efforts and organizational results,
- organizational results and societal (or personal) success and impact,
- what we are to do, how we do it, and the results we achieve,
- MEGA, MACRO, and MICRO payoffs, consequences, and synergies.

And if you want to determine the usefulness of anything resulting from any organizational element, determine if the "fit" among organizational elements is appropriate. Sooner or later, internal and organizational results must have positive external payoffs, or you can do without them.

Useful, systematic planning relates internal resources, efforts, and methods to organizational (in-house) results and contributions to external results and payoffs and, thus, better assures that individual and organizational efforts yield useful OUTCOMES—payoffs in and for today and tomorrow's society.

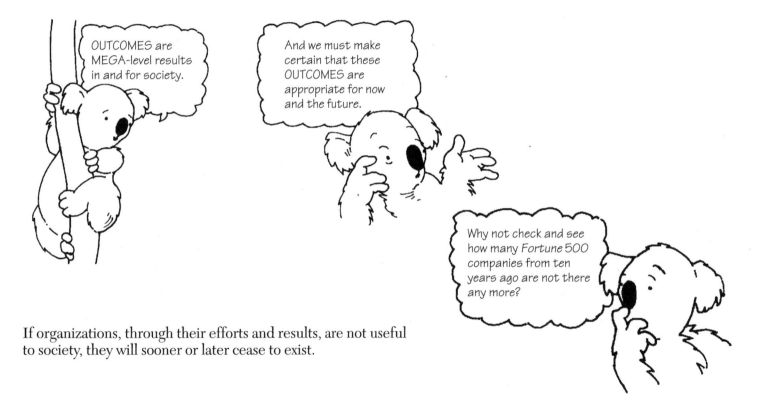

If organizations, through their efforts and results, are not useful to society, they will sooner or later cease to exist.

INPUTS, PROCESSES, and PRODUCTS all contribute to organizational results that are called OUTPUTS. OUTPUTS (it is hoped that they are appropriate and useful) contribute to external results that are called OUTCOMES. We should always try to achieve useful OUTCOMES—positive impact in and for society.

Confusing internal efforts and results with useful external impact and usefulness can bring you unintentional failure!

The ultimate usefulness of MEANS (organizational efforts) and the organizational results they achieve are at the external ENDS (OUTCOMES)/MEGA level.

All the MEANS—the INPUTS and the PROCESSES—and all the internal results—the PRODUCTS and the OUTPUTS—are useful only to the extent that they have utility in the "real" world (external to the individual and the organization)! One way to keep MEANS and ENDS straight is to ask yourself, "If this is the solution, what's the problem?" or, "If my organization is the solution, what's the problem?" Thinking this way would stop single-issue quick-fixes or "analysis paralysis"!

Don't you wish politicians dealt with this?

In problem solving and decision making, no matter who we are, results are important. Why don't we start right now by getting MEANS (INPUTS and PROCESSES) and ENDS (PRODUCTS, OUTPUTS, and OUTCOMES) in the correct perspective? Why not manage for success rather than react to crises?

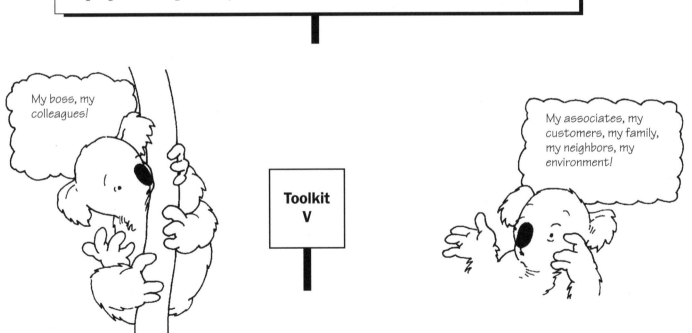

We have just learned that

- IDEAL VISIONS identify the world we want for tomorrow's child;
- If you don't know where you are headed—an IDEAL VISION—you are in jeopardy of heading in the wrong direction;
- An IDEAL VISION provides the MEGA-level results toward which we strive in order to improve;
- The IDEAL VISION provides the basis for your Mission and aligning what you use, do, produce, and deliver;
- MEGA-level results—the IDEAL VISION—provide the basis for what organizations use, do, produce, and deliver.

Four

Where Are We Headed and Why?
Objectives, Measurability, and Needs Assessment

Look at these two statements of current results.

Which statement provides us with more information? Which statement seems most useful? Which statement allows us to determine what results we are now getting and what results we want? Sure, the first one is more helpful (and it is also more precise).

The more precise our measurement is, the more chance we have of
- making sure we are setting meaningful and appropriate objectives;
- making appropriate choices among possible MEANS in order to get from where we are to where we want to be;
- helping us confirm our progress and results;
- having the proper basis for continuous improvement and evaluation.

First, realize that you don't have to measure at all—except when you really want to make a difference! (If you don't care, or don't want to know if you have gone from What Is to What Should Be, then don't measure.) However, if you want to change or make a change, the more precisely you measure, the more you can know

- if you are on the right track,
- if you have been successful,
- what worked,
- what should be changed if you are not successful.

And evaluation is always used for fixing and never for blaming.

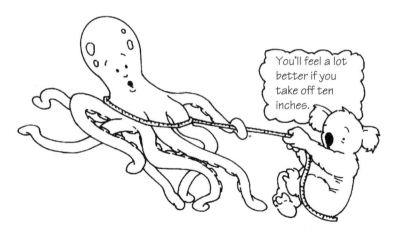

You'll feel a lot better if you take off ten inches.

Measurement and methods and techniques we use for measurement may be likened to other tools. They are amoral, neither good nor evil. You can use a hammer to pound someone into the ground or you can use it to build a temple. The user determines whether a tool is used appropriately. We don't want to do away with all measurement just because some people have misused measurement in the past. Our job is using measurement to help ourselves and our fellow humans as we learn from our performance.

By the way, when we measure, it doesn't always have to be in terms of the familiar statistical means and standard deviation; any time we label something we are, in fact, measuring! In fact, there are four scales of measurement:

- Nominal,
- Ordinal,
- Interval,
- Ratio.

We suggest that the more refined and precise the scale of measurement, the more reliable the measure! Let's see some possible uses for each.

Nominal-scale measures simply name or label.

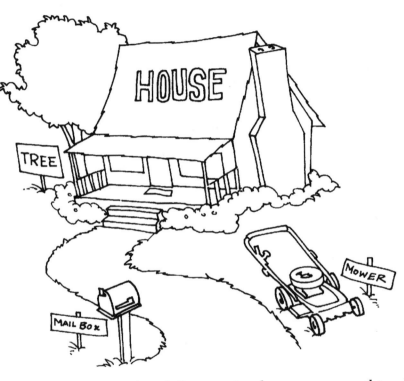

If you can name something, you are measuring! And if you can't at least name something, like "love," "beauty," "quality," etc., then you can't really be sure it exists!

Ordinal-scale measurement involves ranking.

My preference list is

1. steak
2. lobster
3. pizza
4. taco
5. chocolate cake
6. cherry pie
7. hot dog
8. salad with no dressing.

We can't say how much more or less preferred each item is, compared to the others. But, we can rank them in order by some criterion such as personal appeal, taste buds, or appetite. With this type of scale, we can say only that one thing is greater than, equal to, or less than something else.

In everyday language we frequently use Ordinal-scale measurements. For example,

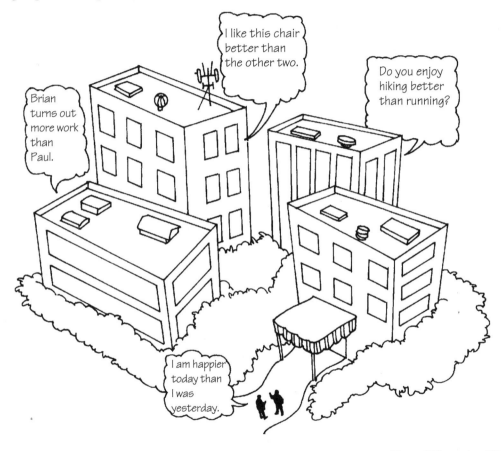

Interval-scale measurements have equal scale distances but an arbitrary zero point. The important thing they tell us is the degree of distance from that arbitrary point. For example,

- maps: the equator and the prime meridian at Greenwich are arbitrary zero points;
- thermometers: 32 Fahrenheit or zero degrees Celsius are arbitrary zero points;
- clocks: midnight is an arbitrary zero point and varies in 24 regions around the world.

We often use Interval-scale measurement in planning human change. Most of our psychological tests, including the ones using those darned means and standard deviations, are Interval-scale measurements. For example, there will be at least 99% fewer accidents attributed to our lawn mower's design as indicated by no successful legal judgments against us as compared to those of other North American firms.

When we want to plan change we are best off if we use Interval-scale measurement or if we use Ratio-scale measurement. Ratio-scale measures feet or pounds as does Interval-scale measurement, except that the zero point really means "zero." It is a starting place that occurs naturally.

Ratio-scale measures are sometimes difficult to apply usefully to human behavior unless we use specific performance criteria such as "There will be no deaths or disabling accidents attributed to our lawn mower design as indicated by no successful legal judgments."

Our four scales for measurement are Nominal, Ordinal, Interval, and Ratio. When we are serious about useful results, it's inefficient to use a less-refined scale of measurement when we have more precise measures that are valid.

It is also inefficient to use a too refined measure when the scale is inappropriate to what we are measuring.

When we set our goals, we are best off if we can state our current results in Interval-scale terms, the most precise scale that generally applies to human behavior. We use measurement when we define our purposes—when we state our Mission or destination.

Setting objectives

Any statement of objectives should include
- what result is to be achieved,
- under what conditions it will be achieved,
- who or what will demonstrate the result,
- what criteria will measure its achievement,
  and will communicate without confusion.

Remember, the more results statements that we can make in Interval and Ratio-scale terms, the better we will be at planning, doing, evaluating, payoffs, and continuous improvement.

Let's look at an example for framing a results statement that will perform the four functions we mentioned previously.

By the time I am 55, the children will have graduated from college and will be out on their own (so that I won't have to contribute money to them.) I will be earning at least two times my age (in thousands of dollars) in a job I like, our home will be paid for, my life partner and I will enjoy more of life's good things, based upon a greater spendable income than what we have now. We will each own a car. We will dine out at least twice per month. We will travel abroad for at least two vacations every five years. We will have season tickets to the symphony. I will have put enough money aside to purchase a small income property (under $200,000) for my retirement. My partner and I will be in "good health" as indicated by a licensed physician's physical examination, and we will stay that way. We will have at least three couples whom we would rate as good friends (or better). We will visit our children frequently (at least twice a year), but not so often that we intrude or interfere, as indicated by their telling us to leave or asking us more than twice in a row not to come.

This is a **MACRO**-level objective.

Notice that this hypothetical What Should Be statement is measurable on an Interval or Ratio scale; identifies who (or what) will display the desired performance and attitudes; lists the criteria for evaluation and the conditions for evaluation; leaves little room for confusion. It does not specify resources of how it will be accomplished, just results.

Let's see how goals and objectives are derived. Goals? Objectives? They are related, but not the same.

Goals set directions. They state where you are headed. Objectives provide criteria to goals for knowing both where you are headed and how to know when you've arrived.

Here is some help: a taxonomy (or hierarchy) of results based upon the precision and reliability of your measures. (34, 35, 39, 52)

Scale of Measurement	Type of Result
Nominal Ordinal	Goal (or aim, purpose, or intent)
Interval Ratio	Objective (or performance specification, or performance indicator)

When you are able to be precise and rigorous about your results, you prepare objectives. When you cannot measure in Interval or Ratio terms, prepare goals. You will help yourself and others if you work on your ability to be precise when writing objectives.

When you are preparing your objectives, aside from making them measurable, also remember to focus on ENDS, not MEANS, or how-to-do-its.

A MISSION Statement defines a destination measurable in Nominal- or Ordinal-scale terms.

For example, "improve quality next year."

A MISSION OBJECTIVE defines a destination measurable in Interval- or Ratio-scale terms.

Every objective at the MEGA/OUTCOME level (an IDEAL VISION), MACRO/OUTPUT level, (MISSION OBJECTIVE), and/or MICRO/PRODUCT level should be in Interval or Ratio terms. Whether you prepare a MISSION OBJECTIVE or a task objective it should be measurable on an Interval or Ratio scale.

Let's see

MISSION STATEMENT + Interval or Ratio criteria = MISSION OBJECTIVE
(intent)   (precise criteria)

or, put another way,

GOAL + Interval or Ratio criteria = objective.

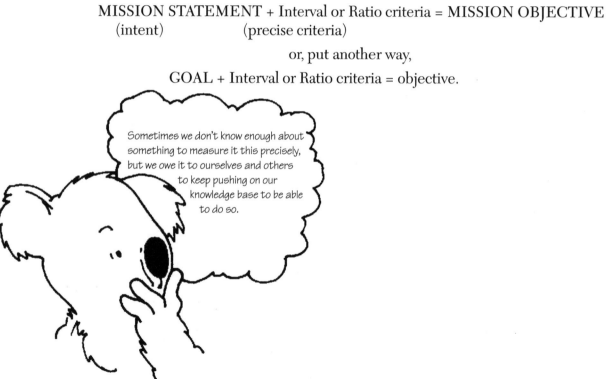

Sometimes we don't know enough about something to measure it this precisely, but we owe it to ourselves and others to keep pushing on our knowledge base to be able to do so.

This measurability of what we do or intend to accomplish on an Interval or Ratio scale is so vital, it is our Critical Success Factor #6.

All objectives, including MISSION OBJECTIVES, should specify both where you are headed and supply the exact criteria for telling when you've arrived.

Reminder, the other Critical Success Factors are
#1: Move out of your comfort zones—today's PARADIGMS—and use new, wider boundaries for thinking, planning, doing, and continuous improvement/evaluating.
#2: Define NEED as a gap in results—between current and desired results—not as insufficient levels of resources, MEANS, or how-to-do-its.
#3: Differentiate between ENDS and MEANS—focus on what before selecting how.
#4: Use and relate all three levels of planning and results—MEGA/OUTCOMES, MACRO/OUTPUTS, MICRO/PRODUCTS.
#5: Use an IDEAL VISION (what kind of world, in measurable terms, we want for tomorrow's child) as the underlying basis for your thinking, planning, doing, and continuous improvement.

Now let's deal with constructing the basis for sensible and sensitive change. Ready?

Whew, we now have all six Critical Success Factors.

If you are getting a certain set of results (PRODUCTS, OUTPUTS, or OUTCOMES) now, and you want to achieve a different or modified set, you should make two parallel lists, a What Is list and a What Should Be list. Pick an area of interest to you and try it out. And note, please, that results may be internal and external and they also relate to PRODUCTS, OUTPUTS, and OUTCOMES.

Check your What Is list and your What Should Be list against our criteria for an objective.

- Do your lists state what OUTCOME (and/or OUTPUT, and/or PRODUCT) is to be achieved?
- Do they state who or what will display the OUTCOME (and/or OUTPUT, and/or PRODUCT) and what criteria will be used to determine its achievement?
- Do they state who or what will display the results and what will be used to measure the achievement?
- Do they avoid ambiguity and confusion?

If they don't meet all these specifications, go back and revise them.

Criteria are most usefully stated in Interval- or Ratio-scale measures.

Results statements, such as this, are called objectives.

Here is an example.

WHAT IS (current results)	WHAT SHOULD BE (desired results)
Earn $26,000 a year at age 39	Earn at least $55,000 a year within 16 years
Pay $950 a month principal and interest on house	Pay off mortgage within 16 years
Paying on one car Net worth of $4,975.00 (no investment program)	Own two cars Net worth of at least $300,000
10% to 15% days per year feeling "sub par" (sporadic health checks when health is poor)	Feel physically "sub par" 5% of the time or less per year (yearly checkups with physician with certification of good health)

You will probably have to have more practice writing measurable results statements. It's worth doing.

Results statements (objectives) may relate to OUTCOMES, OUTPUTS, and PRODUCTS.

Don't get discouraged or lose interest. The trip is worthwhile. Keep at it. Continue to improve as you move toward MEGA-level results and payoffs.

Toolkit
VII

Want to take other people into consideration? Most people aren't alone in the world (although we might feel pretty lonely from time to time), and what we do affects others—and vice versa. So why not take into account these interactions, interrelationships, and shared payoffs?

When we are selecting goals and objectives, we can involve our partners in NEEDS ASSESSMENT.

Each partner, or group of partners, can (and really should) fill out a What Is and What Should Be statement.

Let's say you are doing educational or training planning and you have, at least, the following partners: recipients—people receiving results, trainees, etc.; associates—partners, co-workers, teachers, administrators; society—clients, parents, legislators, regulators, citizens, etc.

Include a What Is and What Should Be analysis for each group.

	What Is (Results)	What Should Be (Results)
Recipients		
Associates		
Society		

Remember to make all statements measurable on an Interval or Ratio scale.

Remember, a **NEED** is a gap between What Is and What Should Be in terms of results.

One possible way to keep MEANS and ENDS separate is to list both MEANS and ENDS along with the possible methods and MEANS, as we have them below.

What Is (Current Results)	Possible Methods and MEANS to get from Is to Should Be	What Should Be (Desired Results)

The MEANS are how you meet or reduce a NEED—how you get from current to desired results.

Now, the purpose of going through all this is to do a NEEDS ASSESSMENT.

A NEEDS ASSESSMENT is a formal process that
- identifies and documents the gaps between current results and desired results, ideally those concerned with gaps in OUTCOMES—or linked to them;
- arranges the gaps (NEEDS) in order of priority;
- selects the NEEDS to be resolved.

A NEED selected for closure is termed a "Problem."

When you list the gaps in results between What Is and What Should Be for you and your partners, you can reconcile any differences (or mismatches) by collecting additional data, using common sense, negotiation, or just plain, rational reasoning.

Agreement comes easier when you discuss ENDS, agree on those first, and then discuss MEANS.

Remember, this is what Critical Success Factors #2 and #3 were about.

NEEDS ASSESSMENT is the first step in improving decision making. It is essential to useful planning. It assures us that where we are headed is where we should be headed, and further, that our partners agree! And whenever people agree about a shared destination, they can then agree on how to get there.

NEEDS ASSESSMENT is purposive, humane, and practical.

And I'm beginning to see how it might work.

Before moving from identifying NEEDS to how to resolve them, here is one more aspect of assessing NEEDS and of relating NEEDS to possible MEANS and resources for achieving success!

We must define What Is and What Should Be for each of the organizational elements.

Let's divide the Organizational Elements Model (OEM) further into What Should (or Could) Be and What Is.

	MEGA/ OUTCOMES	MACRO/ OUTPUTS	MICRO/ PRODUCTS	PROCESSES	INPUTS
WHAT SHOULD OR COULD BE				↕	↕
WHAT IS					

The "What Should Be's" are best derived from the IDEAL VISION—contribute to MEGA-level results.

In conducting an assessment, we could move from the precise measurable (in Interval- or Ratio-scale terms determination of What Should (or Could) Be for each element, and then, do the same for What Is.

	MEGA/ OUTCOMES	MACRO/ OUTPUTS	MICRO/ PRODUCTS	PROCESSES	INPUTS
WHAT SHOULD OR COULD BE					
WHAT IS					

Once we have done that, then we may determine (and justify) NEEDS by entering our data into the OEM.

The three types of NEEDS are in the shaded portions.

	MEGA/ OUTCOMES	MACRO/ OUTPUTS	MICRO/ PRODUCTS	PROCESSES	INPUTS
WHAT SHOULD OR COULD BE					
WHAT IS					

Notice that there are three types of results, and thus there are three types of NEEDS—gaps in results—and three types of NEEDS ASSESSMENTS.

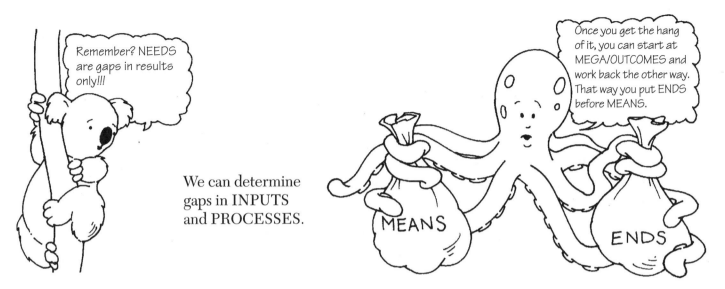

	MEGA/ OUTCOMES	MACRO/ OUTPUTS	MICRO/ PRODUCTS	PROCESSES	INPUTS
WHAT SHOULD OR COULD BE					
WHAT IS					

Gaps in PROCESSES as well as gaps in INPUTS are really QUASI-NEEDS. (It doesn't make sense to close gaps in resources or methods unless they will close gaps in results. If we don't pick MEANS on the basis of meeting NEEDS, just what do we have in mind?)

To complete a rigorous (and practical) NEEDS ASSESSMENT, you determine NEEDS and QUASI-NEEDS for each of the organizational elements.

EVALUATION CRITERIA: A hidden bonus in Needs Assessment.

The "What Should Be" variable of your NEEDS ASSESSMENT will provide you with continuous improvement/evaluation criteria. By defining a NEED as a gap in results you get a bonus—you already have your evaluation criteria in place. The OEM will serve to guide you on what to keep and what to change, and will provide Rational justification as well.

Oops! This means a "training NEEDS ASSESSMENT" really deals only with Quasi-Needs.

Then, for each organizational element, you determine change requirements; determine continuation requirements or that which should be left alone (then you will be able to close the gaps, knowing what the real NEEDS are); identify possible interventions and how-to-do-its (MEANS); and then you select interventions. You may prioritize the NEEDS—gaps in results—by answering, "What does it cost to meet the NEED?" versus "What will it cost to ignore it?" You can also demonstrate value added.

Using NEED as a gap in results, you can justify any proposal based on results and consequences. If someone turns down your request, simply ask him or her to take responsibility for <u>not</u> meeting the needs.

Some call that cost-results or cost-consequences analysis.(31, 38)

Keep in mind that not all NEEDS and problems arise from a gap within an existing system or organization. Sometimes there are gaps in societal results to which no existing organization is currently responsive. A new organization might be considered, to help close the gaps. Or you might discover a market niche others have overlooked. Therefore, two assumptions you should stay away from are "My organization can solve all problems" and "Needs are deficiencies, not discrepancies." Why?

Organizations are existing MEANS to societal ENDS. We might want to create new organizations or change some existing ones, based on NEEDS. NEEDS ASSESSMENT may identify gaps in results, be they too little or too much of something. Keep in mind that NEEDS are discrepancies and not necessarily deficiencies.

What?

There are two sources of NEEDS data:

- perceptions concerning gaps in results ("soft" data) and
- actual performance concerning gaps in results ("hard" data).

Both are useful in identifying and selecting NEEDS.

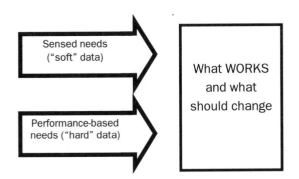

We can compare the hard and soft data to make sure they agree. If they don't agree, collect more data, ask different-but-related questions, and keep digging until you get agreement.

Once you have identified, documented, justified, prioritized, and selected NEEDS and QUASI-NEEDS, you are ready to get from What Is to What Should Be.

Time to review what we've learned.

- Realistic direction (or purpose) setting defines destinations in precise, rigorous, measurable terms.
- Purposes deal only with ends, with results.
- When objectives are precise and measurable, they provide realistic evaluation criteria.
- There are four scales of measurement, Nominal, Ordinal, Interval, and Ratio.
- If you can name something, you are measuring it. Therefore, everything is measurable.
- All objectives target ENDS and never include means or resources.
- Objectives state where you are headed and provide the criteria for knowing when and if you've arrived.
- NEEDS are gaps in results.
- NEEDS ASSESSMENT identifies the gaps in results and places them in priority order.
- There are three levels of results, and thus three possible levels for NEEDS ASSESSMENT.
- An assessment of gaps in INPUTS and/or PROCESSES are QUASI-NEEDS ASSESSMENTS.

- NEEDS data include "soft" (personal, nonobjective) and "hard" (independently verifiable) data. Both are vital.
- NEEDS are prioritized on the basis of what it costs to meet the NEED as compared to the cost to ignore it.
- The gap between What Is and What Should Be defines a NEED as a gap in results; the What Should Be dimension provides you with the evaluation criteria.
- Goals are measurable on a Nominal or Ordinal scale.
- Objectives are measurable on an Interval or Ratio scale.
- There are six Critical Success Factors (10, 11) that will keep your problem solving and strategic thinking practical and useful.
  ▶ Critical Success Factor #1: Move out of your comfort zones—today's PARADIGMS—and use new, wider boundaries for thinking, planning, doing, and continuous improvement evaluating.
  ▶ Critical Success Factor #2: Define NEED as a gap in results—between current and desired results—not as gaps in resources, the MEANS, or how-to-do-its.
  ▶ Critical Success Factor #3: Differentiate between ENDS and MEANS—focus on what before selecting how.

- Critical Success Factor #4: Use and relate all three levels of planning and results—MEGA/OUTCOMES, MACRO/OUTPUTS, MICRO/PRODUCTS.
- Critical Success Factor #5: Use an IDEAL VISION (what kind of world, in measurable terms, we want for tomorrow's child) as the underlying basis for your thinking, planning, doing, and continuous improvement.
- Critical Success Factor #6: All objectives, including MISSION OBJECTIVES, should both specify where you are headed and supply the exact criteria for telling when you've arrived.

Five

How to Get From Here to There— The Bridge to Success: Applied Problem Solving, a Six-Step Process

The Management Plan—What's to be accomplished to get from What Is to What Should Be

The management plan (34) is best shown as a series of PRODUCTS displayed within rectangles that depict the order of, and the relationships between, the en route PRODUCTS.

This is actually a problem identification and resolution process!

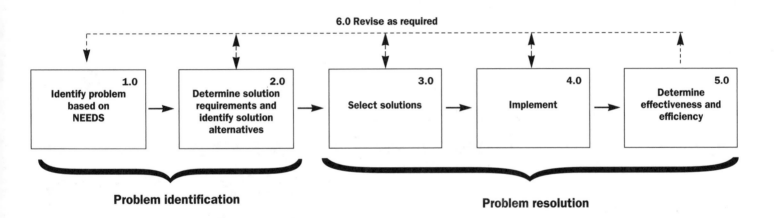

This is an example of a most general problem-solving process model. Let's take a closer look at each PRODUCT.

The first PRODUCT is

> **1.0**
> **Identify problem**
> **based on NEEDS**

This is a trade-off between what we give and what we get!

You have accomplished this when you have identified the gaps (NEED) between current OUTCOMES and desired OUTCOMES (or any gap in results). Don't worry if it looks linear. It is not; many of the steps can go on at the same time.

If you've done what was suggested previously, you have
- listed gaps between current results and desired results and
- selected—on the basis of what it costs to meet versus the costs to ignore—NEEDS, or gaps in results that have the highest priorities.

You know where you are and where you want to be.

Now it is time to
- perform an analysis to determine all the requirements (specifications) necessary to get from here to there;
- identify possible ways and means to get you there in the quickest and easiest manner, so that later you can select the best ways and MEANS;
- assure yourself that the "trip" is feasible.

With that accomplished, we are ready to shift from the external objectives to internal objectives; determine the possible ways and means to get from here to there; and plan and accomplish the internal objectives.

We hope you start with an IDEAL VISION.

This builds a bridge for getting from current results to desired results—moving from What Is to What Should Be.

Toolkit
VII

The first thing to do is use your What Should Be statement as an overall statement of OUTPUT (or result): What your organization will deliver to external clients.

This is called the **MISSION OBJECTIVE.**

A MISSION OBJECTIVE states results at the MACRO level.

The **MISSION OBJECTIVE** (or overall results statement) should be written in terms of measurable performance. For example,

Within five years, the Ideal Ice Cream Company (or its surviving organization) will show a positive return on investment, as certified by independent audit, and will achieve external success, as indicated by at least a 10 percent increase in per-share stock-market price compared to the price one year earlier. In addition, within two years, the employees of the Ideal Ice Cream Company will have developed a positive attitude toward the firm, as indicated by at least a 90 percent drop in absenteeism and employee turnover, a 99 percent reduction in lost orders, and an equal drop in spillage and loading-dock damage. There will also be a substantial (at least 70 percent) increase not only in the number of positive suggestions from employees to management, but in those submitted and used. There will be a readiness to discuss problems openly instead of grumbling among small groups, as measured by an absence of strikes, slowdowns, or stoppages. On its side, management will recognize problems when they arise and will move to solve them at once. This will alleviate escalation into major and bitter issues and will make union contract negotiations at the end of two years easier, as measured by a reduction in contract disputes.

From this **MISSION OBJECTIVE**, construct a management plan of what (regardless of what **MEANS** are used to get there) "en route" **PRODUCTS** are to be achieved to get you from What Is to What Should Be.

Here's an example.

Ideal Vision	MEGA level/OUTCOMES
Mission Objectives	MACRO level/OUTPUTS
Functions and Building Block Results	MICRO level/PRODUCTS

The second PRODUCT in this problem solving process is to

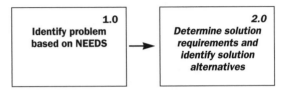

| 1.0 Identify problem based on NEEDS | → | 2.0 Determine solution requirements and identify solution alternatives |

Here all the requirements for getting from What Is to What Should Be are analyzed, and alternative ways and MEANS to meet these requirements are identified but not selected.

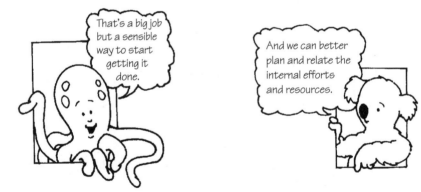

The NEEDS ASSESSMENT identified gaps in results and selected problems; this step analyzes them—like trouble-shooting.

From your What Should Be statement (MISSION OBJECTIVE) you then develop a management plan showing each function in your overall plan. The overall plan for identifying and solving any problem, called a MISSION PROFILE, looks like this.

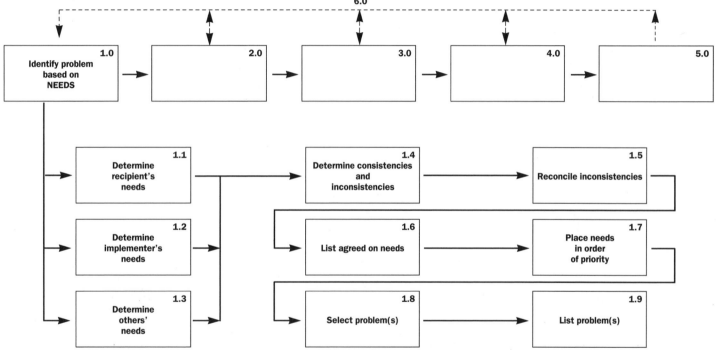

Any overall problem identification and resolution plan that includes the basic functions to be performed and shows the order and relationships among the functions (or PRODUCTS) is called a MISSION PROFILE.

A MISSION PROFILE can be developed for identifying and resolving any problem. It may be developed for a very general area (such as the six-step process for identifying and resolving any problem) or it may be developed for a very specific problem, such as achieving the MISSION OBJECTIVE for the Ideal Ice Cream Company.

Each function (or PRODUCT) in the MISSION PROFILE has a number with a zero after the decimal point: 1.0, 13.0, 14.0, etc. This is a cue to everyone that it is a Function at the MISSION PROFILE level.

A MISSION PROFILE may be developed to get from What Is to What Should Be for any one (or combination) of the Organizational Elements. The process of developing a "mini-management plan," or "break-out," is called function analysis. Each mini-plan has a number related to its functions, such as: 1.2, 1.3, 1.9, 1.1.1, 1.9.1, 1.9.2.

Each Function is a PRODUCT—it identifies a result to be delivered.

The different names and numbers locate differences in levels of planning. For example, 1.1, 1.2, 1.9 all derive from the higher function of 1.0. Likewise, 1.1.1 derives from function 1.1.

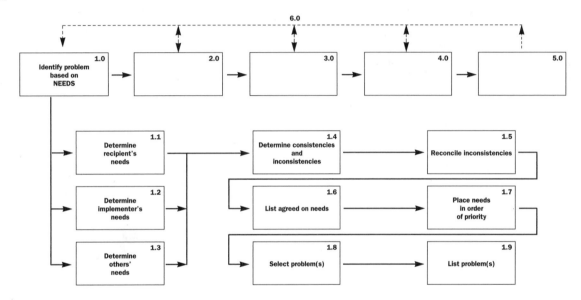

What does this function analysis tell you? Put into words, it says, in order to identify the problem, based on NEED (1.0), you

1.1 determine the recipient's NEEDS, and
1.2 determine the implementer's NEEDS, and
1.3 determine the others' NEEDS, and then
1.4 determine those NEEDS about which there is agreement or disagreement,

1.5 reconcile the inconsistencies (you might later elect to negotiate, convince, obtain additional data, etc.), then

1.6 list the NEEDS about which there is agreement, then

1.7 place the NEEDS in order of priority, then

1.8 select the problem(s) to be worked on (a problem is a NEED selected for resolution), and then

1.9 list the selected problem(s).

I have to remember that NEEDS are gaps between current results and desired results, not PROCESSES or resources.

Next, do a break-out (function analysis) for each element in the overall plan (MISSION PROFILE) on as many levels as necessary to define all the important requirements and interrelationships.

This is really using the six-step process for each function in the overall management plan.

Because you can always revise as required, this is not a rigid approach.

Each time you identify a function, list measurable specifications (OBJECTIVES) for the accomplishment of each one and identify possible ways and MEANS for meeting each specification.

The identification of possible ways and MEANS is accomplished without selecting how-to-do-its (MEANS or resources) in order to consider alternatives and keep the options open!

The first two steps (1.0 and 2.0) of the management plan—or MISSION PROFILE—are concerned with planning and the balance (3.0, 4.0, and 5.0) are concerned with doing (what you've planned).

Of course, continuous improvement/evaluation—comparing our desired results with our accomplishments—is ongoing.

The Third Product in this problem solving process is

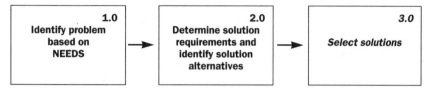

| 1.0 Identify problem based on NEEDS | 2.0 Determine solution requirements and identify solution alternatives | 3.0 *Select solutions* |

That means to select the most effective and efficient ways and means of meeting the requirements, thus moving from What Is to What Should Be.

The Fourth Product is

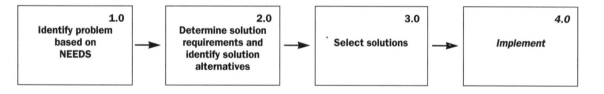

| 1.0 Identify problem based on NEEDS | 2.0 Determine solution requirements and identify solution alternatives | 3.0 Select solutions | 4.0 *Implement* |

Implement means doing what you planned (in 1.0 and 2.0), using the ways and means you selected in (3.0).

The Fifth Product is

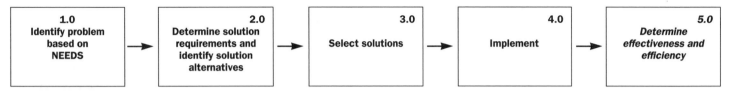

That means determine how well or how poorly the requirements have been met.

The Sixth Product is

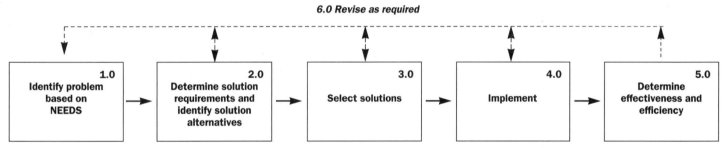

Revise as required means make changes any time and any place in your planning and doing process when you are not getting where you want to be. This is a self-correcting process. Changing as required and when required as you move from What Is to What Should Be is called formative evaluation. This is very much like continuous improvement. Changing on the basis of the end-of-program results is called summative evaluation. Evaluation (the process and findings from Products 5.0 and 6.0) data are used for continuous improvement, never for blaming.

This six-step problem solving process is a basic tool that is useful any time you want to identify and resolve problems!

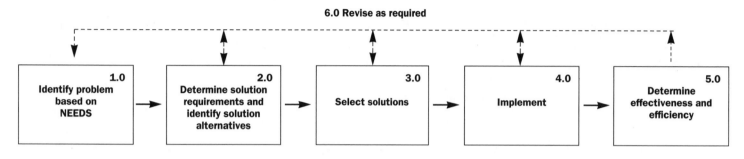

Short cycle times make us do this rapidly, even doing some of the steps at the same time!

Let's apply it to our example.

Let's go back to our original MISSION OBJECTIVE.

Within five years, the Ideal Ice Cream Company (or its surviving organization) will show a positive return on investment, as certified by independent audit, and will achieve external success, as indicated by at least a 10 percent increase in per-share stock-market price compared to the price one year earlier. In addition, within two years, the employees of the Ideal Ice Cream Company will have developed a positive attitude toward the firm, as indicated by at least a 90 percent drop in absenteeism and employee turnover, a 99 percent reduction in lost orders, and an equal drop in spillage and loading-dock damage. There will also be a substantial (at least 70 percent) increase not only in the number of positive suggestions from employees to management, but also in those submitted and used. There will be a readiness to discuss problems openly instead of by grumbling among small groups, as measured by an absence of strikes, slowdowns, or stoppages. On its side, management will recognize problems when they arise and will move to solve them at once. This will alleviate escalation into major and bitter issues, and will make union contract negotiations at the end of two years easier, as measured by a reduction in contract disputes.

Using this What Should Be statement, draw a plan (MISSION PROFILE) for getting from where you are to the accomplishment you want.

This statement has all the characteristics of an objective.

Perhaps it would look like this.

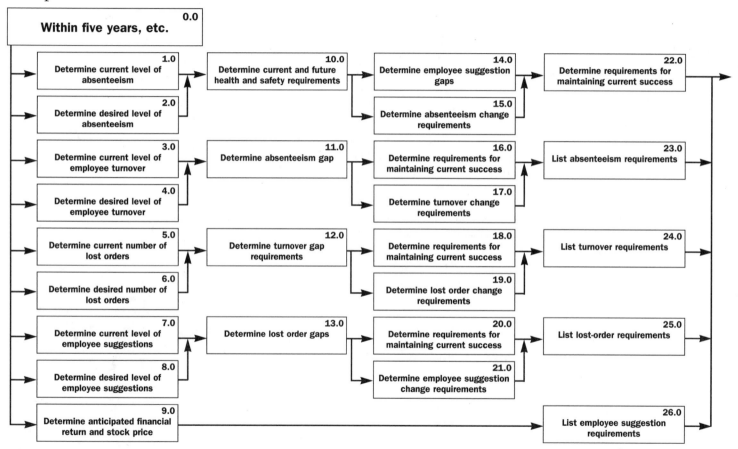

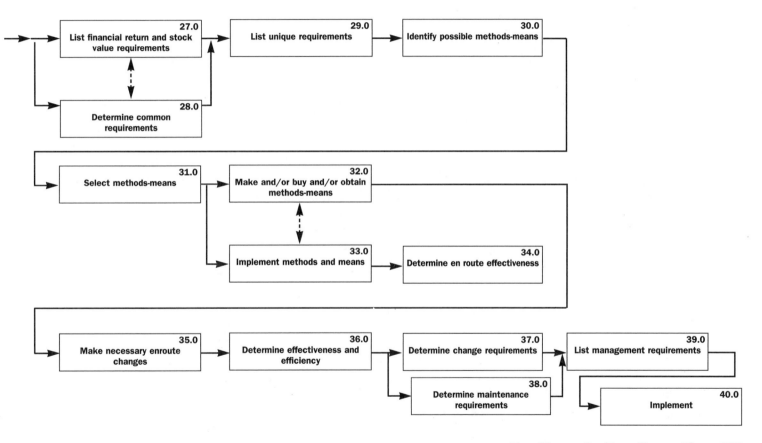

Continue this analysis until you are certain that if you did what you planned, you would get from What Is to What Should Be!

Then, identify possible ways and MEANS for accomplishing each Function. Here is a possible (but hypothetical) methods and MEANS analysis for function number 8.0.

FUNCTION	POSSIBLE WAYS AND MEANS	ADVANTAGES	DISADVANTAGES
8.0 Determine current number of employee suggestions	A. Ask top-level supervisors B. Ask lower level supervisors C. Random sampling of employees in each department D. Analyze recent contributions to suggestion boxes	A. Fast B. Closer contact with workers on the floor C. First-hand information D. Factual	A. Too far removed from workers on the floor B. Personal bias enters in C. Might exaggerate their contributions D. Often impossible to tell the number of employees submitting suggestions

This is called Methods-Means Analysis.

You now have the necessary information for successful planning.

- An overall OBJECTIVE (MISSION OBJECTIVE) that is best derived from an IDEAL (MEGA level) VISION.
- A management plan for getting the OBJECTIVE accomplished (MISSION PROFILE plus function analysis).
- Alternative ways and means for implementing the plan, including a list of the advantages and disadvantages of each.
- The assurance of feasibility (if you hadn't found any ways and means, you would know you couldn't accomplish the MISSION OBJECTIVE).

You are now ready to go from planning to doing!

You are applying a systematic process for identifying and resolving problems.

Here is what we've covered in Applied Problem Solving.

- A system approach process has six steps:
  - identify problems based on NEEDS,
  - determine solution requirements and identify solution alternatives,
  - select solutions (from among alternatives),
  - implement,
  - determine effectiveness and efficiency, and
  - revise as (and whenever) required.
- This six-step process is the basis for a management plan (called a MISSION PROFILE).
- The first two functions are concerned with planning, the balance with doing.
- The six steps, in some form, are useful any time you identify and resolve problems, at the MEGA, MACRO, and/or MICRO levels.

Six

Decisions, Decisions: Using All of the Tools

Some people like to make decisions, others avoid them. Either way, decisions get made!

In problem solving using the previous planning and the resulting information, you still have to make decisions, but now it is easier and it is safer because you have all of the facts to justify your decisions.

There goes my comfort level again. Not making a decision is a decision.

Basically, you can make a wise, and practical, selection if you
- know where you are going (**MISSION OBJECTIVE** based on **NEEDS**), and know why you want to get there,
- know what has to be accomplished to get from where you are to where you want to be, and
- know the alternative ways and **MEANS** (how-to-do-its) to get from here to there.

And if you've followed along until now, you have all of the required information.

Wait a minute? How *do* I sort out all those alternatives?

Making useful decisions simply involves asking (and answering) two simultaneous questions, "What do I give?" and "What do I get?" In other words, what it costs to get the desired results as compared to what it will cost not to get them.

Just relating costs and results, almost sounds too sensible and reasonable.

List the alternative ways and MEANS you have for doing the job, or getting from where you are to where you want to be and select the best ones on the basis of the answer to this question, "What is the highest (or best) payoff for the lowest investment?" Don't put it off, because not making a decision, is a decision.

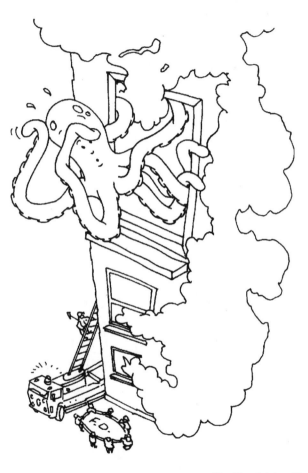

For example, here is a sample costs-results analysis.

ALTERNATIVE	COST	RESULT/BENEFIT
1. Spend vacation visiting our friends, the Websters	1. A. $75 for travel B. Sleep on sofa-bed C. Have to see their tedious friends D. Have to eat the Websters' cooking	1. A. Have money left after vacation B. Get to see old friends C. Get a partial vacation
2. Go to San Juan	2. A. $1,355 travel expense B. Minimum room and board $150 C. Nervous when flying D. Will have to borrow and repay $1,000 E. Maybe only meet new people I wouldn't want to meet	2. A. Vacation will be novel B. Have good memories C. Meet new people
3. Stay home	etc.	etc.

What do we now possess so that we may make useful decisions?

- A MISSION OBJECTIVE—in precise measurable terms—that states where we are headed and how to tell when we've arrived.
- The MISSION OBJECTIVE that links to an IDEAL VISION of what our organization (and everyone involved) is to deliver. This will result in a payoff for both our clients and shared world.
- The results of a NEEDS ASSESSMENT that identifies and prioritizes the gaps in results on the basis of what it costs to meet the needs as compared to the costs for ignoring them.
- A management plan (or MISSION PROFILE) that uses a six-step problem solving process for identifying what should be delivered, then what alternative methods and means are available for meeting the NEEDS, and then selected solutions based on costs-results analysis.
- OBJECTIVES for each function—the building-block results for getting from What Is to What Should Be—to use for both design and evaluation.

Our decisions may now be made on rational, defensible data. The tools, and the results of using them, include

- a practical and useful focus on tomorrow's world—the IDEAL VISION;
- a MISSION OBJECTIVE out of which come building-block results;
- functions to be completed;
- methods-means identified;
- criteria for determining success.

Decisions are best made with valid data and a shared destination. The application of the tools and methods allows you to have confidence in your decisions and to do practical, strategic thinking.

The most powerful process you can use in making decisions—what this book really focuses on—is the six-step problem solving process.

When you have to make decisions, follow these six steps.

1. Identify problems based on NEEDS;
2. Determine solution requirements and identify alternatives;
3. Select solutions (from among alternatives);
4. Implement;
5. Determine performance effectiveness and efficiency; and
6. Revise (whenever) as required.

These six steps should be applied any time you want to identify and resolve problems—in short, when you want to make decisions that will deliver useful results. If you want to take unnecessary risks, don't use all six steps or don't use them in the correct sequence. All of the tools, processes, and techniques provided in this guide are useful for applying one or more of the six steps of identifying and resolving problems. Use them.

Is such a rational approach realistic?
Some do object. "Isn't this all overly rational and 'hard nosed?'"
"Does the world really work in such a linear and lock-step
manner? Isn't this approach unrealistic?" "What about
humanism, values, and cooperation?"

Sorry, if it appears to be rigid, lock-step, and linear. It really isn't
like that. It is wise to ask these questions. We don't want to make
the process rigid.

This approach is sensible, practical, and rational, not rigid. It is
also humane and humanistic, and gets that way through
inclusion of all by empowering everyone to participate in the
identification and resolution of problems. It allows us to act
dynamically, synergistically, and rapidly.

This approach to identifying and resolving problems does invite
all partners—those who can and might be affected by whatever
results are defined and delivered—to help define where it is we
should head. It involves others, not excludes them. We care
enough about people to ensure their success, and to include
them in doing so.

It really is human networking—we all define where to head and know when to revise.

The structure of our six-step problem solving process allows—even insists—on responsiveness and continuous evaluation and change. Remember the sixth step, "revise as, and whenever required"? This keeps the whole process responsive. It requires that we make continuous and ongoing decisions about where are we headed, should we be headed there, are we making appropriate progress, and are we making necessary changes to ensure that we are not only headed toward the correct destination but also making continuous and required progress?

When this approach is used appropriately (it won't work if we misrepresent what we're doing), we are responsive and responsible as we define where to head and then decide how best to get there. We define the necessary criteria for sensible, sensitive, and useful decision making. It is humane, humanistic, practical, and pragmatic. When we use this approach to strategic thinking, we in fact have decided to succeed!

And that's what it's all about!

Seven

Doing What You've Planned—Well

You can see that when you are making decisions about personal goals and objectives, your selection of one option among many may be rather subjective. When you are in more precise areas like business, science, and technology, you can do actual pragmatic cost/results studies. Whether you do a formal cost-consequence analysis, which is usually best, or an informal one, your decision is your first affirmative-action step.

You have already
- defined where you are and where you want to be;
- identified all the steps to be accomplished;
- identified possible optional ways and means to get there, plus listed the advantages and disadvantages of each; and
- selected the most effective and efficient how-to-do-its.

So you know what you are going to do and how you are going to do it. Your next job is to do it!

You are now ready for Operational Planning and Doing. (34, 39) Make, buy, build (or beg, borrow, or liberate) the tools and resources for getting the job done and schedule resources. Make sure that what you will be using will be ready and waiting when you have to use it.

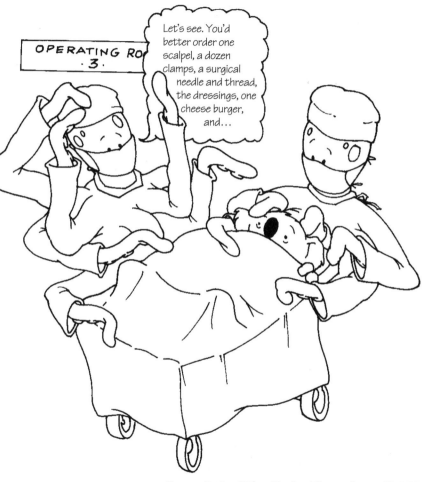

Some activities are best carried out when we make out a schedule of time, events, and interrelationships.

Some simple schedules consist of a chart, called a Gantt Chart, like the one below.

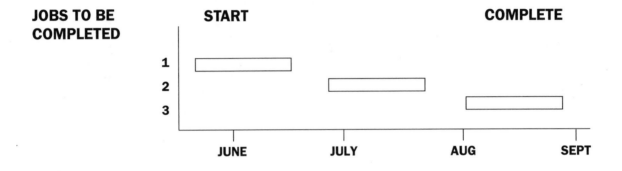

More complex charts may use flow charts like the one below.

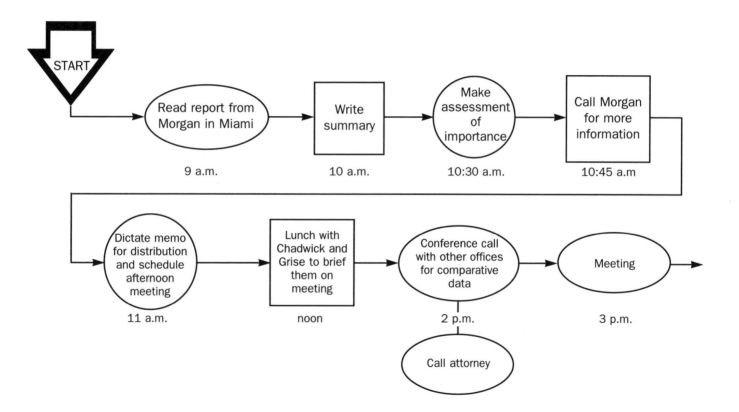

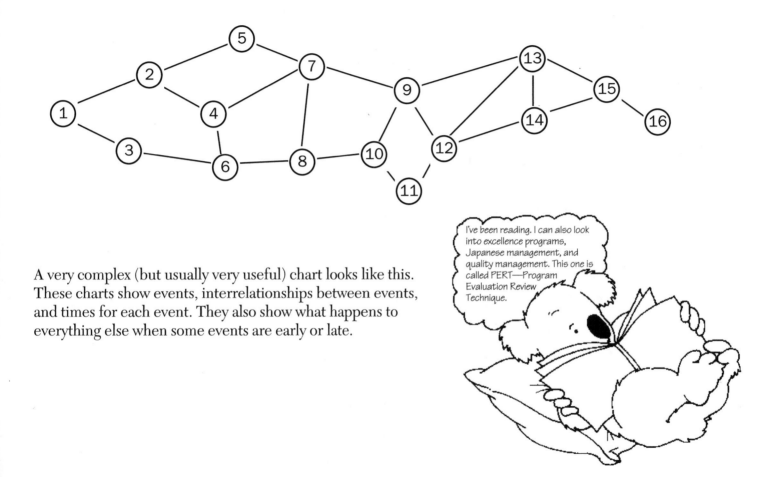

A very complex (but usually very useful) chart looks like this. These charts show events, interrelationships between events, and times for each event. They also show what happens to everything else when some events are early or late.

I've been reading. I can also look into excellence programs, Japanese management, and quality management. This one is called PERT—Program Evaluation Review Technique.

Regardless of how you organize it all, you are now in operation and moving toward success, and that requires

- precise objectives,
- timing,
- commitment,
- sensing and adjusting, and
- orchestrating yourself and your resources.

Good management for getting from What Is to What Should Be is working smarter, not just working harder.

That's good life-management, too!

Eight

Finding Out How You Did
and
Revising as Required

Remember earlier how much of a fuss was made about measurement and measurability? We stated, in measurable terms, where we were going. Now the measurable criteria tell us how to know when we've arrived. We can compare our accomplishment with our objectives, our results with our intentions.

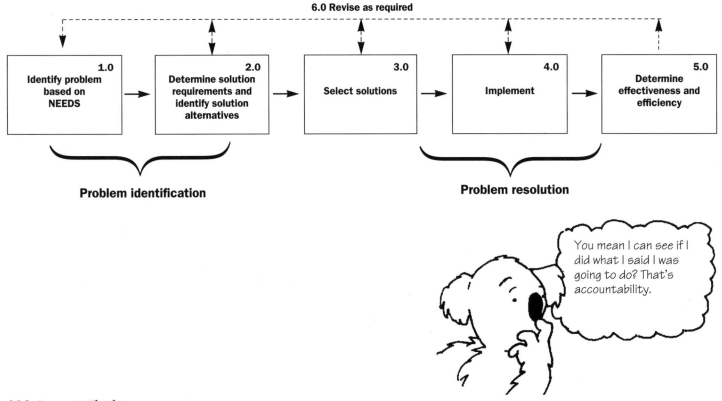

So let's compare by using our MISSION OBJECTIVE from page 126.

OBJECTIVE	SUCCESS OR FAILURE
A) Positive return on investment	A) Success
B) 10 percent share increase in stock	B) Failure
C) 90 percent drop in absenteeism and employee turnover	C) Success
D) 99 percent reduction in lost orders	D) Success
E) Increase in employee suggestions used	E) Failure
F) Management reducing contract disputes	F) Success

This step allows you to see how well or how poorly you have accomplished what you set out to do. In our hypothetical example, we would maintain our performance on objectives A, C, D, and F. We would revise our procedures for objectives B and E. We might question the validity of our gap (NEED) on employee suggestions. Go back to the data collected for functions 7.0, 8.0, 14.0, 21.0, 22.0, 26.0, 28.0, 29.0, 30.0, 31.0, 32.0, 33.0, 34.0, 35.0 (Mission Profile on pages **129** and **130**) to assure their correctness and make whatever changes might be necessary.

Evaluation and continuous improvement can be your best friend. It will tell you where you were successful and where you should make changes—where renewal should take place.

While you are solving a problem and when you have completed the problem-solving process, you should always learn from any mistakes. Use the information about the gaps between that which you have accomplished and that which you have not accomplished. But never use evaluation data for blaming—only for fixing and improving!

Unfortunately, we aren't always successful in doing everything we set out to do.

Therefore your job, both here and throughout, is to revise as required whenever and wherever you have not accomplished what you set out to accomplish.

Each time you achieve a result, determine if you are "on target" and, if not, where you should revise. Because all your objectives are written in measurable terms, you can, at any point, see where you are off target. Whenever you are not getting from What Is to What Should Be, you should go back and redo what is necessary to be successful.

This process can achieve renewal of the system.

You can do a number of things if you are not getting from What Is to What Should Be:

- Change the objective(s),
- Find another way to try to meet the objective(s), or
- Quit.

Usually, changing the objective will result in your not meeting the original NEED! But, it is worth checking your NEEDS to make sure that they are still appropriate. Things change fast, and you want to be "on top" of reality constantly.

Things do change fast: the Internet, Asia's emergence, high-performance computing.

Most often, you should look for other ways and MEANS to meet your unmet objectives, so move back to the second product. (It is in the detailed solution requirements and possible alternatives that failures most often may be turned into successes.)

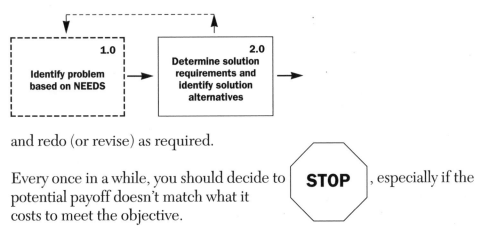

and redo (or revise) as required.

Every once in a while, you should decide to **STOP**, especially if the potential payoff doesn't match what it costs to meet the objective.

If you do stop, however, go back to your NEEDS ASSESSMENT and start all over again. In fact, you might want to redo the entire Organizational Elements Model analysis for all of the What Is's and What Should Be's.

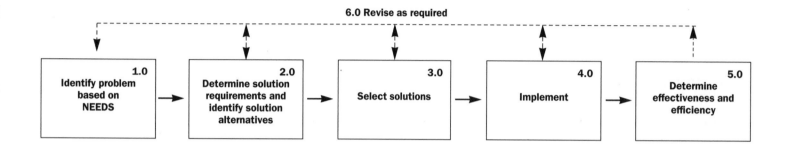

The last stop of this problem-solving process (like NEEDS ASSESSMENT) is a constant, ongoing procedure. It allows us to be self-correcting in order that decisions to change will assure success.

Nine

So?
Putting the Tools to Work

**HERE IT IS!
THE HIGHEST SPOT—
YOU MADE IT!**

We have just hit the high spots of a PROCESS for successful decision making. A System Approach to identifying, justifying, and resolving problems and a systematic approach for strategic thinking.

A System Approach has two parts.

- One identifies "What Is" and "What Should Be" (determines NEEDS) for defining and delivering useful results, and
- One determines and delivers what must be accomplished in order to get from What Is to What Should Be.

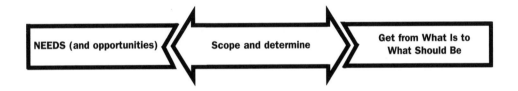

The Organizational Elements Model (OEM) is used to scope the areas of NEED and to document What Is and What Should Be for the societal impact, organizational results (MACRO- and MICRO-level results), and organizational efforts (INPUTS and PROCESSES).

	MEGA/ OUTCOMES	MACRO/ OUTPUTS	MICRO/ PRODUCTS	PROCESSES	INPUTS
WHAT SHOULD OR COULD BE					
WHAT IS					

The six-step problem solving process is used to identify what must be accomplished in order to resolve any problem. It builds the bridge between What Is and What Should Be, and thus meets the NEEDS that have been identified, justified, and selected for resolution.

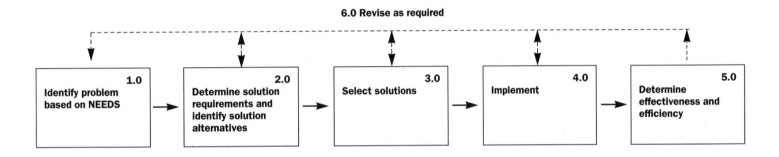

You may use the six-step problem solving process for any one (or combination) of the organizational elements.

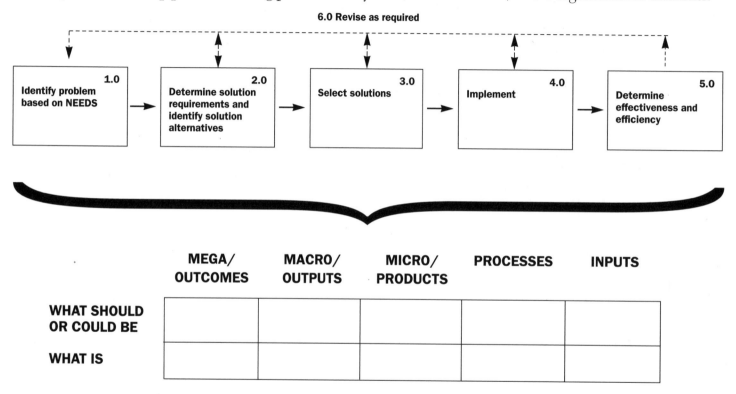

6.0 Revise as required

Identify problem based on NEEDS 1.0	**Determine solution requirements and identify solution alternatives** 2.0	**Select solutions** 3.0	**Implement** 4.0	**Determine effectiveness and efficiency** 5.0

	MEGA/ OUTCOMES	MACRO/ OUTPUTS	MICRO/ PRODUCTS	PROCESSES	INPUTS
WHAT SHOULD OR COULD BE					
WHAT IS					

...Any time you want to determine gaps between

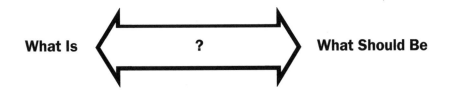

What Is ? **What Should Be**

...and close those gaps

Strategic Thinking and Strategic Planning Plus will allow you to define What Should Be for results and plot the pathways to success.

Toolkit X

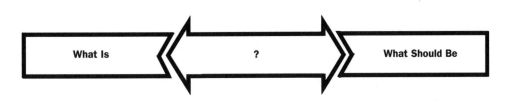

What Is ? What Should Be

The OEM will allow you to

- separate (and relate) MEANS and ENDS;
- list What Is and What Should Be for each element;
- determine NEEDS (gaps in results) to be closed;
- determine QUASI-NEEDS (gaps in resources or methods) to be closed; and
- relate everything to move ever closer to the IDEAL VISION.

Then the six-step problem solving process will be a useful tool for

- determining a MISSION OBJECTIVE and specifications for getting from What Is to What Should Be;
- identifying a major (MISSION PROFILE) management plan plus minor (Function Analysis) management plans to list what has to be accomplished and in what order it must be finished;
- listing possible ways and MEANS to accomplish each function;
- selecting the best tactics and tools;
- showing what must be done to successfully implement the selected tactics and tools;
- determining the overall effectiveness and efficiency; and
- revising wherever and whenever required.

Another process that fits very well with this is Quality Management (QM). (25, 37)

Briefly, the processes for QM cluster into three groups: a passion for quality, everyone on the same team, and data-based decision making as you and everyone else moves continuously toward client satisfaction (and the IDEAL VISION.)

Toolkit XI

The QM process builds on, and uses, all of the six Critical Success Factors as it

- defines quality (measurable specifications for the IDEAL VISION, your mission, and all products);
- involves and empowers everyone as they, together, move toward the mission;
- maps the pathways from "What Is Quality?" to "What Should Be Quality?"
- uses the data from NEEDS ASSESSMENT and OBJECTIVES to select ways and means to consistently deliver quality;
- continuously improves the processes as it moves closer and closer to achieve quality specifications and client satisfaction;
- decides what to continue, what to modify, and what to stop as everyone continuously improves.

Toolkit IX

QM is a means to defining and delivering useful results.

If you add MEGA-level results to your QM process you further assure that the continuously improved processes will contribute to both client satisfaction AND societally useful results.

So this is called "QM+."

The Organizational Elements Model and the six-step problem solving processes together may be used as partners to identify and solve important problems. It provides a System Approach to manage your success.

Quality Management processes will help you and your partners get the results you want.

You may use the six-step problem solving process for any one (or combination) of the organizational elements.

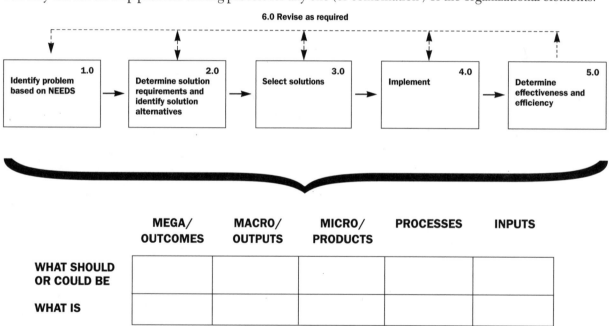

QM and QM+ provide the process for continuous improvement as we move from What Is to What Should Be.

...All in terms of results.

Toolkit
XI

The six-step process identifies problems and opportunities that allow you to be responsive and responsible. NEEDS ASSESSMENT identifies the gaps in results to be closed. Evaluation, using the What Should Be dimension from the NEEDS ASSESSMENT, identifies what works and what doesn't. The QM process provides the continuing "engine" for change and for continuous improvement. The QM (and QM+) process will, when consistently applied, ensure that useful results will be achieved and will allow us to move ever closer to our IDEAL VISION.

Quality Management (and QM+) provides the process for continuous improvement as we move from What Is to What Should Be.

Your successes will exceed your failures, and you will improve continuously if you use the problem solving approach provided here. You will see that your efforts will be effective, efficient, humane, practical, and useful.

And you can be proactive; you can create the future for you and your organization—define MEGA and move ever closer to it.

GETTING IN THE LAST WORD

You should now have the basic concepts and tools for making useful decisions that lead to success. No idea or concept is useful if it is not put into action, so try these ideas and see that they work. The tools for identifying and solving problems are available to serve you. One-shot problem solving may be useful in the short run, but for best results, use these tools continually to identify and solve problems. Quick fixes usually have to be refixed.

Remember that these processes can be changed and modified to suit your individual situation. They will serve you only if you decide to use them.

**Toolkit
XI**

The pilot is on course now.

So just do it!

Part 2: The "Hows" of Strategic Thinking and Planning

Toolkits I–XI

STRATEGIC THINKING AND PLANNING TOOLKIT

Whereas the first part of this book provides the basics of strategic thinking, planning, identifying, and resolving problems, this part shows how to make these concepts come alive and improve your organizational and professional success. Its aim is to help you implement the concepts and tools presented in this book.

A Toolkit is designed to
- help define the scope of strategic thinking;
- relate strategic thinking and planning to identifying and resolving problems; and
- identify some of the key tools and processes for improving organizational success.

In the first part of the book, each time there is appropriate applications material, a sign is provided telling you which Toolkit section will help. The concepts and definitions presented in the first part of the book are not repeated in the Toolkit.

The framework and approach suggested here is different from conventional methods. Because our world has changed, simply working harder and harder (or, as Peter Drucker notes, "getting better and better at doing what should not be done at all") will not serve us well. The conventional understandings will fail us. (2, 3, 4, 5, 13, 14, 16, 24 ,32, 34, 35, 39, 43, 45 ,49, 51)

In our new context of a changed world with changed realities, very powerful tools such as strategic planning, Total Quality Management, needs assessment, benchmarking, and reengineering can fail us for the wrong reasons. The basic concepts and the potential payoffs for planning and doing are far too important to allow them, individually or together, to achieve less than success. Problems can arise, for you and your clients, from inconsistent application, incomplete or inappropriate models, improper management and administration, failure to integrate and find the synergies among them, or not being responsive to new demands on our cycle-time. We no longer have the luxury of waiting to develop linear responses and must act almost simultaneously to all areas of change. This Toolkit builds on the concepts presented. It provides guidance on how to help you and your internal and external clients to define and achieve success.

Toolkit I

Needs Assessment

<table>
<tr>
<td>
</td>
<td>
A NEEDS ASSESSMENT identifies the gaps between current and desired results and places them in priority order on the basis of what it costs to meet the NEED versus what it costs to ignore it. It is vital to define NEED as a gap in results and never as a gap in resources or methods (called QUASI-NEEDS). (26, 29, 35, 36, 38, 39, 55)

It is often useful to examine an existing NEEDS ASSESSMENT effort and PRODUCTS to find out how complete and appropriate it is. (The Organizational Elements Model and its uses are also provided in Toolkit III.)
</td>
</tr>
</table>

Here is an activity for assessing your NEEDS ASSESSMENT.

Exercise 1.1

Use a NEEDS ASSESSMENT that you have either used, developed, or experienced.

1. Examine the NEEDS ASSESSMENT and identify which elements of it
    • identify a NEED as a gap in results,
    • identify a QUASI-NEED—a "NEED" as a gap in methods or a gap in resources.
2. For each NEED identified, classify it as
    • MEGA/OUTCOMES-related,
    • MACRO/OUTPUTS-related, or
    • MICRO/PRODUCTS-related.
    Note the NEEDS listed for each results level. Anything missing?
3.   For each QUASI-NEED (gaps in processes and/or resources), ask "if I did or delivered this, what result would I get?" Continue to ask that question until you have identified NEEDS at the three levels of results. List them.

4. Using the NEEDS ASSESSMENT Audit below, review an existing NEEDS ASSESSMENT and identify if it is likely to be useful and appropriate. If the reviewed NEEDS ASSESSMENT does not meet the basic criteria, what changes should be made?

Note: Most existing NEEDS ASSESSMENTS are really oriented to identifying MEANS and resources desired—more of a "wish list"—and assume that obtaining the MEANS and resources will deliver useful results. This audit is designed to help you identify what is useful and what might be missing from any NEEDS ASSESSMENT.

You may use a brief audit (based on 22, 23) to determine how complete and responsive a NEEDS ASSESSMENT might be.

A NEEDS ASSESSMENT Audit

Use the following as a checklist. You can rate each item on a yes or no basis using the criteria for your judgment.

CRITERIA	YES	NO
1. NEEDS are identified as gaps between current results and desired results (or stated another way, the gap in results between "what is" and "what should be").		
2. There is a clear distinction made between ENDS (results, consequences, payoffs) and MEANS (resources, methods, how-to-do-its).		
3. There are three levels of results identified, one for societal and client contributions (MEGA level), another for organizational contributions (MACRO level), and one for individual performance (MICRO level).		
4. The three levels of results include the MEGA level (results, payoffs, consequences) for external (outside of the organization) clients.		
5. MEGA-level results are clearly related to an IDEAL VISION for the kind of world we want for tomorrow's' child (not just on the purpose of the organization alone).		
6. The three levels of results include the MACRO level (results, payoffs, consequences) for the organization itself.		

CRITERIA	YES	NO
7. The MACRO-level results are clearly related to required results and consequences at the MEGA/IDEAL VISION level—MACRO results contribute to moving ever closer to the IDEAL VISION and the MEGA-level results and payoffs.		
8. The three levels of results include the MICRO level (results, payoffs, consequences) for individuals and/or small groups within the organization.		
9. The MICRO-level results are clearly related to delivering required results at the IDEAL VISION, MEGA, and MACRO levels of results.		
10. Any statement of NEED is free from any indication of how the NEED will be met (such as training, computers, technology).		
11. Any statement of NEED is free from any indication of what resources will be used to meet the NEED (such as personnel, time, money, equipment, etc.).		
12. NEEDS are listed in priority order on the basis of what it costs to meet the NEED versus what it will cost to ignore it.		
13. Interventions are selected on the basis of a Costs-Consequences Analysis for each NEED, or cluster of related NEEDS.		
14. Continuous Improvement (Evaluation) criteria are taken directly from the "what should be" dimension of the selected NEEDS.		
15. Continuous Improvement (Evaluation) results report the extent to which NEEDS, or families of related NEEDS, have been reduced or eliminated.		
16. Continuous Improvement (Evaluation) results are used for fixing and not for blaming.		

Note: Most existing NEEDS ASSESSMENTS are really oriented to identifying MEANS and resources desired (a "wish list") and assume that getting the MEANS and resources will deliver useful results. This exercise and NEEDS ASSESSMENT audit are designed to help you identify what is useful and what might be missing from any NEEDS ASSESSMENT. As you review NEEDS ASSESSMENT, notice that most of them are often only wants ASSESSMENTS. Instead of identifying gaps in results, they attend to deficiencies in MEANS (such as training courses) or resources (personnel, computers, funds).

NEEDS ASSESSMENT Data: Do They Relate to NEEDS?

Here is a hypothetical example (although these are all based on findings of so-called NEEDS ASSESSMENTS I have seen) of the results of a NEEDS ASSESSMENT done by Fuzzy Worldwide Industries.

Fuzzy Worldwide Industries' NEEDS ASSESSMENT Findings:

1. We have to have managers managing with vision.
2. We have to be world class.
3. We have to be competitive.
4. We NEED to have more executive training.
5. We NEED to cut down on training time.
6. We NEED to make quality "job one."
7. We must all work together.
8. We must increase our production by 18%.
9. There must be no injuries or deaths from what we deliver.
10. We must make a profit each year.
11. We must not pollute the environment, so that there will be no loss of life, loss of species, or illness or incapacity from pollution.

Compare your results with these:

1. We have to have managers managing with vision.

   This is a MEANS (Process). It states nothing about what results and payoffs there will be from "managing with vision," nor does it state what the vision will be.

2. We have to be world class.

   This aspiration never defines what "world class" is or how we would measure it. It also does not state what the results and payoffs will be from being "world class." This does not relate to a NEED but is an intention, and a fuzzy one at that.

3. We have to be competitive.

   This aspiration never defines what "competitive" is or how we would measure it. It also does not state what the results and payoffs will be from being "competitive." This does not relate to a NEED but is an intention, and—like #2—another fuzzy one.

4. We NEED to have more executive training.

   This is a MEANS. Your first clue that it is, is the use of "NEED" as a verb and that dumps one into MEANS without defining the ENDS to be accomplished. In this case, what gap in results would be closed by "more executive training"? What gap in results would this deliver at the MICRO, MACRO, and MEGA levels?

5. We NEED to cut down on training time.

   This is also a MEANS. Your first clue, once again, is the use of "NEED" as a verb; again, that dumps one into MEANS without defining the ENDS to be accomplished. In this case, what gap in results would be closed by "cutting down on training time?" What gap in results would this deliver at the MICRO, MACRO, and MEGA levels?

6. We NEED to make quality "job one."

   This is a MEANS. Again, there is the use of "NEED" as a verb that shunts one into MEANS without defining the ENDS to be accomplished. In this case, what gap in results would be closed by "making quality job one"? What is "quality," and how do we measure it? What gap in results would this deliver at the MICRO, MACRO, and MEGA levels?

7. We must all work together.

   This is also a MEANS. In this case, what gap in results would be closed by "working together"? What gap in results would "working together" deliver at the MICRO, MACRO, and MEGA levels?

8. We must increase our production by 18%.

   At last! A result: a MICRO-level one. If it were stated as a NEED—a gap between current results and desired ones—it might be stated, "current production is at X, and we will increase it to at least Y, an increase of production of at least 18%."

9. There must be no disabling injuries or deaths from what we deliver.

   This will deliver results at the MEGA level. If stated as a NEED, it might read, "Last year there were three disabling injuries and one death from our OUTPUTS. Next year and following there will be no disabling injuries and no deaths from our OUTPUTS."

10. We must make a profit each and every year.

    This will deliver results at the MEGA level, to the extent to which profit is earned without bringing harm to anyone or to the environment. Profit over time is an indicator of a MEGA-level contribution. Continuing to show a profit over time is an indicator both of the usefulness of what you deliver and of customer satisfaction. No quick-fix profits here, where one puts out something cheap and disappears in the dark of night before the quality of what was delivered is discovered. If stated as a NEED, it might read, "Last year we had a loss of $2.23 million. Next year and following we will show a profit each and every year."

11. We must not pollute the environment so that there will be no loss of life, loss of species, or illness or incapacity from pollution.

    This will deliver results at the MEGA level to the extent that what Fuzzy Industries does and delivers does not bring harm to people and the environment; they are "good neighbors." If stated as a NEED, it might read, "Last year we had two spills cited by the environmental council as toxic and destructive. Starting next year and following we will have no legally cited incidents causing toxic damage or other kinds of personal or environmental destruction."

Notice that none of Fuzzy Worldwide Industry's NEEDS were stated as gaps in results. This is a common mistake, and one you can avoid. NEEDS, if they are to be useful for identifying what is working and what is not, must be defined as gaps in results.

A NEEDS ASSESSMENT Summary Format

Table 1.1 provides a form for summarizing NEEDS ASSESSMENT data. Sort your NEEDS data into this and note that there is a column for current results and desired results. The form also has a column for possible solutions so that suggestions that are made may be considered (and dignified) in terms of the gaps in results they might close. Also, there are columns for identifying the result level of a NEED (MEGA/OUTCOMES, MACRO/OUTPUTS, MICRO/PRODUCTS.)

NEEDS and the Three Levels of Results

NEEDS may (and should) be identified at the three levels of planning (MEGA, MACRO, and MICRO) and the three related levels of results (OUTCOMES, OUTPUTS, PRODUCTS). If the NEEDS at each level are not linked—they contribute to each other—then we might have interventions at the MICRO level that will not make a positive contribution up the results chain: MICRO to MACRO to MEGA. Figure 1.1 is a job aid to use to check these linkages.

				NEED Level		
Current Results	Possible MEANS	Desired Results	Referenced IDEAL VISION Element	MEGA	MACRO	MICRO

Table 1.1 A NEEDS ASSESSMENT summary format. (based on 35, 36, 39, 40)

Missions: Are they appropriate?

Mission Elements:

a)

b)

c)

    etc....

Target		ENDS Level		
MEANS	**ENDS**	**MICRO**	**MACRO**	**MEGA**

Steps:
1) List each element of the mission.
2) For each, determine if it relates to a MEANS or an END.
3) If an element relates to an END, determine if it is focused at the MICRO, MACRO, or MEGA level.
4) If an element relates to a MEANS, ask "What result would I get if I got or accomplished this?" Keep asking the same question until an END is identified.

A format and procedure for assuring that your mission is useful, deals with ENDS and not MEANS, and has MEGA-level expectations.

Figure 1.1 A job aid for ensuring that NEEDS relate to ENDS and also to link the three levels of planning and results.

Collecting NEEDS ASSESSMENT Data

There are two kinds of NEEDS ASSESSMENT data, "hard" and "soft." A NEEDS ASSESSMENT should collect two kinds of data, soft (personal and not independently verifiable judgments of NEEDS based on perceptions) and hard (objective performance data that can be externally validated). The two sources of data should agree before selecting a NEED for reduction or elimination. If there is disagreement, go back and collect more data. Also, be certain that the data collected is not biased. Don't only ask questions or collect data that are convenient to get or that support what you want to see as a result.

Whether collecting hard or soft NEEDS ASSESSMENT data, the focus should be on results and not on MEANS, PROCESSES, or resources.

One way to obtain "soft" data is through structured interviews with planning partners—those who will be impacted by whatever gets planned and delivered as well as those who will deliver whatever gets planned—concerning the gaps between current results and desired ones. Also useful are questionnaires concerning the gaps in results.

One useful format for questionnaires is to get responses on results-related questions in terms of both What Is and What Should Be. In one approach, planning partners are invited to respond to a series of questions using a seven-point scale (ranging from zero or not at all, to perfect or completely). The scale values can vary for individual applications.

What Is (seven-point rating scale)							Question (results-related)	What Should Be (seven-point rating scale)						
1	2	3	4	5	6	7		1	2	3	4	5	6	7
							All deliveries are on time							
							All deliveries meet customer requirements							
							There are zero customer complaints							
							Associates are 100% competent in all • skills • knowledge • attitudes • abilities							
							There are no deaths or disabilities from what we deliver							
							Our work place is completely safe							
							There are no negative environmental impacts from our work							
							There are no negative environmental impacts from our OUTPUTS							
							All trained associates make a contribution to their • work assignment • organization's OUTPUTS • external client success • societal well-being							

Objective, independently verifiable data are usually easier to obtain than commonly believed. There are What Is data easily accessible for societal impact (MEGA) performance including the health, safety, and well-being of citizens and customers from chambers of commerce, US Departments of Commerce and Labor, as well as state agencies. You can usually find other data for each element of the Organizational Elements Model, including data about your organization from your organization. Such data could include sick leave rates, legal actions (both successful and not), and the like. Local, state, and federal data sources abound, as do local and state information. When you are collecting hard and soft data, be sure that they relate to your specific objectives and that all three levels of results are included.

Toolkit II

Ensuring That You and Your Organization Are Headed in the Right Direction

The basic questions every organization must ask and answer

Whether we realize it or not, every organization faces the questions listed below. (36, 40)

Do you commit to deliver organizational contributions that have positive impacts on and for society? (MEGA/OUTCOMES)

Do you commit to deliver the contributions that have quality required by your external clients? (MACRO/OUTPUTS)

Do you commit to produce internal results that have the quality required by your internal clients? (MICRO/PRODUCTS)

Do you commit to having efficient, internal organizational programs, projects, and activities used in your organization? (PROCESSES)

Do you commit to create and ensure the quality and appropriateness of the human, capital, and physical resources available to your organization? (INPUTS)

Do you commit to deliver
- the positive value and worth of your activities, methods, and procedures?
- the results and accomplishments defined by your objectives? (Evaluation/Continuous Improvement)

To help orient yourself and others in your organization, the following exercise may be useful.

Exercise 2.1

Using the "Basic Questions Each Organization Must Ask and Answer," please do the following:
1. Which of the questions do you think your organization and any of your internal (associates within your organization) and external (customers, citizens, neighbors, society) clients can afford not to address formally and in rigorous and measurable terms?

LEVEL OF STRATEGIC PLANNING AND THINKING and TYPE OF RESULTS	CAN AFFORD NOT TO ADDRESS FORMALLY	MUST ADDRESS FORMALLY
MEGA/OUTCOMES		
MACRO/OUTPUTS		
MICRO/PRODUCTS		
PROCESSES		
INPUTS		
CONTINUOUS IMPROVEMENT (Evaluation)		

2.   Which of the questions do you believe your organization and any of your internal and external clients do or do not formally and completely address in precise, rigorous, and measurable performance terms?

LEVEL OF STRATEGIC PLANNING AND THINKING and TYPE OF RESULTS	DO NOT ADDRESS FORMALLY	DO ADDRESS FORMALLY
MEGA/OUTCOMES		
MACRO/OUTPUTS		
MICRO/PRODUCTS		
PROCESSES		
INPUTS		
CONTINUOUS IMPROVEMENT (Evaluation)		

3.   What are the risks for starting at the MEGA level? What are the risks of not starting at the MEGA level? The usual pattern found in organizations around the globe is as follows:

A. What levels of strategic planning and thinking should organizations attend to?

LEVEL OF STRATEGIC PLANNING AND THINKING and TYPE OF RESULTS	CAN AFFORD NOT TO ADDRESS FORMALLY	MUST ADDRESS FORMALLY
MEGA/OUTCOMES	No	Yes
MACRO/OUTPUTS	No	Yes
MICRO/PRODUCTS	No	Yes
PROCESSES	No	Yes
INPUTS	No	Yes
CONTINUOUS IMPROVEMENT (Evaluation)	No	Yes

B. What levels of strategic planning and thinking do we now formally and rigorously attend to?

Note: Most organizations feel that addressing MEGA might initially get some people out of their comfort zones, but the costs in terms of organizational failure (and probable loss of jobs) far outweigh the initial risk of beginning all planning at the MEGA level.

C. What value are you now adding? What value should you be adding at the MEGA, MACRO, and MICRO levels?

LEVEL OF STRATEGIC PLANNING AND THINKING and TYPE OF RESULTS	CAN AFFORD NOT TO ADDRESS FORMALLY	MUST ADDRESS FORMALLY
MEGA/OUTCOMES	Agree	No
MACRO/OUTPUTS	Some	Some
MICRO/PRODUCTS	Some	Some
PROCESSES		Yes
INPUTS	Some	Some
CONTINUOUS IMPROVEMENT (Evaluation)	Some	Some

Ensuring the linkages between interventions and contributions to organizational purposes and external payoffs and consequences

Whenever considering any intervention—training, benchmarking, workplace layout, reengineering—first check to assure that whatever will be done will contribute to each of the three levels of results, PRODUCTS, OUTPUTS, and OUTCOMES. The following is a format (and sequence) to use to check to assure these linkages.

MEGA/OUTCOME Objective(s)   **(Societal)**
MACRO/OUTPUT Objective(s)   **(Organizational)**
MICRO/Product/Operational Unit Objective(s)
Individual Performance Objective(s)
Alternatives Considered
Activities/Programs/Projects/Interventions

Table 2.1 A format and procedure for linking any intended intervention to organizational and societal payoffs and consequences.

For each of these levels of results and consequences, you may identify the gaps between current results (NEEDS) and required ones as well as checking for the gaps in PROCESSES and INPUTS. The format in Table 2.2 will shape those activities and link them to results and consequences.

What Is (Results)	What Should/Could Be (Results)
MEGA/OUTCOME Objective(s) (Societal)	
MACRO/OUTPUT Objective(s) (Organizational)	
MICRO/Product/Operational Unit Objective(s)	
Individual Performance Objective(s)	
Alternatives Considered	
Activities/Programs/Projects/Interventions	

Table 2.2 A format for NEEDS ASSESSMENT and QUASI-NEEDS ASSESSMENT for intended interventions.

Strategic Planning Framework

When using strategic planning, a three-phase framework is recommended. (34, 35, 39, 39)

LEVEL OF STRATEGIC PLANNING AND THINKING and TYPE OF RESULTS	CAN AFFORD NOT TO ADDRESS FORMALLY	MUST ADDRESS FORMALLY
MEGA/OUTCOMES	Agree	No
MACRO/OUTPUTS	Some	Some
MICRO/PRODUCTS	Some	Some
PROCESSES		Yes
INPUTS	Some	Some
CONTINUOUS IMPROVEMENT (Evaluation)	Some	Some

Figure 2.1 A strategic planning plus framework. (34, 35, 38, 39)

This strategic planning framework has three phases, Scoping, Planning, and Implementation and Continuous Improvement. Notice that there is no specific and formal function in this strategic planning and thinking process for identifying beliefs and values (as is so often seen in conventional strategic planning models). Developing an IDEAL VISION requires people to confront their beliefs and values (usually closely held and rarely objectively questioned) in the context of identifying and defining the kind of world they want to help create for tomorrow's child.

This recommended strategic planning (and thinking) framework will allow the development of strategic, operational, and tactical plans that will move your organization ever closer to its own survival and success while making a positive societal contribution. (10, 11, 12, 14, 31, 34, 35, 38, 39, 45, 46, 48, 49, 51)

The essential phases and elements of Strategic Planning Plus (SP+). Referring to Figure 2.1, each of the three phases and associated elements are very briefly described. Using this framework will likely lead to positive organizational and societal consequences of what is planned and delivered. Tools and guidance for doing most of the steps of SP+ are in this Toolkit as well as in the references supplied in this book.

I. SCOPING

1. Select the MEGA level as the scope for strategic planning from among three result-level alternatives. The MEGA-level option includes MACRO and MICRO within it. When you select MEGA, you get the others automatically. The MEGA level is the most practical and pragmatic choice because the simple reality is that our organizations are means to societal ends.

2. Derive the IDEAL VISION. Basic to selection of the MEGA level is the development of a results-based statement of a shared IDEAL VISION. At this Scoping step, the planning partners identify and define "what should be" and "what could be" in terms of an ideal society. Deriving a shared IDEAL VISION allows the partners to compare their beliefs and values with the IDEAL VISION. The comparison of one's beliefs and values (often really only biases and stereotypes) with the definition of what kind of world we want for tomorrow's child provides them the opportunity to revise old beliefs and values based on the IDEAL VISION.

3. Define current mission. While working on steps 2 and 4, you will obtain the current mission, and, as is usually necessary, it will be rewritten in results terms. These revisions will include developing measurable indicators of "where we are headed," and "what criteria will allow us to certify when we have arrived?"

4. Identify NEEDS. Using the definition of a NEED as a gap between current and desired/required results, and employing both performance and perception data, the gaps between current results and desired results are identified (starting with gaps for the IDEAL VISION). (In a later step we will use this to identify NEEDS in years, such as year 2010, 2000, 1998, etc.) The importance of conducting a NEEDS ASSESSMENT—the identification and prioritizing of NEEDS—that defines "need" as a gap between current and desired/required results—is basic and fundamental. NEEDS are rationally prioritized on the basis of "what it costs to meet the NEEDS versus what it costs to ignore them."

5. Identify the primary MISSION OBJECTIVE. At this point in Strategic Planning Plus, the primary MISSION OBJECTIVE (including detailed performance criteria) is derived. It is based on the part of the IDEAL VISION the organization commits to deliver[1] and to move toward continuously. The MISSION OBJECTIVE will serve as the basic direction in which your organization will head, a guiding North Star. It states the MACRO-level results (OUTPUTS) to be delivered. If one selects a primary MISSION OBJECTIVE that is not derived from the MEGA/IDEAL VISION level, one risks the entire enterprise. If one does not intend to contribute to getting continually closer to the IDEAL VISION, what are his or her intentions? Is he or she willing to risk the conduct of an entire organization that does not contribute to creating a better world?

The primary MISSION OBJECTIVE is based on a comparison between current intentions (the results-defined current mission) and desired results (based on the IDEAL VISION and the meeting of priority NEEDS) in order to define what it will take to get from "what is" to "what should be," or from current results to desired ones. A mission statement identifies destination intentions that are measurable only on a Nominal or Ordinal scale.

Mission statement + interval/ratio scale criteria = MISSION OBJECTIVE.

---

[1]Of course, no individual or single organization can deliver world peace or no deaths from crime. But one may commit to deliver that to current and potential clients of the organization.

II. PLANNING

The PRODUCTS of completing the Scoping elements provide the basis for building the strategic plan.

1. Identify SWOTs: Strengths, Weaknesses, Opportunities, and Threats. The objective unearthing and consideration of the organization's strengths, weaknesses, opportunities, and threats—SWOTs—are accomplished and analyzed, usually through both internal and external scanning of the inside and outside organizational environments. Future trends as well as opportunities are identified and documented. While many are tempted to only examine weaknesses and threats, this step allows the identification of possibilities that might otherwise remain obscure.

2. Identify long and short-term missions. Based on the shared IDEAL VISION, identified NEEDS, the primary MISSION OBJECTIVE, and the SWOTs, select the building-block—long- and short-term destinations—MISSION OBJECTIVES. These linked en route MISSION OBJECTIVES—from the year 2010 to 2000, from 1998 to next year—contain the measurable specifications for the organization in terms of their OUTPUTS (what are the quality characteristics of what will be delivered to external clients and thus also society). These long- and short-term missions build a results bridge between current results and the achievement of the primary MISSION OBJECTIVE.

These building-block MISSION OBJECTIVES are based on trend data and what is currently known and possible. The SWOTs information from step 2 provides a data base for the determination of the long- and short-term missions.

The primary MISSION OBJECTIVE, based on the IDEAL VISION and the building-block missions, identify the results that the organization commits to deliver. Also, the MISSION OBJECTIVES provide the criteria for en route missions that will bridge from this year to that future (year 2010 mission, year 2000 mission, etc.). The ladder of MISSION OBJECTIVES also provides the basis and criteria for determining progress of the organization and for Continuous Improvement opportunities.

At this step, the planning partners frequently have to go back and collect new and different data that came from the statement of the IDEAL VISION and NEEDS as compared with the existing mission. A continuing emphasis on the difference-yet-relationship between ENDS and MEANS is vital.

Operational, or en route, milestone results—called functions—for implementation are set, along with the identification and selection (from alternatives) of the tactics and approaches (methods-MEANS) to be used. The functions may be arrayed to form a management plan—called a mission profile—that identifies the results to be accomplished and the order in which they should be completed.

Strategic plans should not be long or complex. Ten pages are about right for most organizations. Tactics and operational plans, which should be based on the strategic plans, best form a separate document. These are based on strategic plans and also usually contain budgets, personnel requirements, and resource requirements.

III. IMPLEMENTATION, EVALUATION/CONTINUOUS IMPROVEMENT

1. Put the strategic plan to work. The activities and results of this last step include the following:

(a) Developing a tactical plan—defining and selecting the best ways and means to deliver the results required in the strategic plan. The tactical plan includes the specifications for designing methods, MEANS, and resources, justifying what is to be accomplished, and how it will be done on a costs/consequences basis. During this step, you may both identify what should be delivered through your organization as compared to other interventions and other delivery agencies (using such approaches as reengineering and benchmarking) and consider alternative tools, techniques, and methods.

(b) The development of an operational plan. The operational plan defines the details of getting all of the tactics (methods-MEANS) delivered including the developing (or acquiring) of the resources, implementation of what has been planned, conduction of formative evaluation, and revision as required while implementation is being carried out. This differs from a tactical plan in that a tactical plan identifies the steps for the how-to-do-its, including the development of time lines for accomplishing each product and delivering it to where it has to be and when it has to be there.

(c) Implementation—putting the plans to work and tracking progress in order to change what is not working, and continuing what is working. Quality Management provides the process for Continuous Improvement to deliver useful results. When used consistently and properly, exceptional results occur.

It takes some time to arrive at these Implementation and Continuous Improvement elements especially because you've had to complete all of the previous steps in this strategic planning framework. But now, all of the requirements are justified on the basis of

- an IDEAL VISION that defines the world for tomorrow's child;
- gaps in results (NEEDS);
- priority NEEDS to be reduced or eliminated;
- MISSION OBJECTIVES that identify the results to be accomplished to get from current results to the achievement of the IDEAL VISION;
- measurable performance specifications and for functions (building-block results) against which alternative methods-MEANS (including curriculum and instruction) may be considered and selected on the basis of a costs/results analysis.

This last SP+ phase includes summative evaluation where purposes (goals and objectives) are compared with results. Based upon the Evaluation/Continuous Improvement—comparing results with intentions—decisions are made about what to continue and requires revision. In addition, the Evaluation/Continuous Improvement criteria are directly taken from the What Should Be portion of the NEEDS ASSESSMENT.

Strategic thinking and planning are ongoing PROCESSES. By using them, you and your organization can create the future.

Toolkit III

The Elements of a Minimal Ideal Vision and Possible Indicators for Each

Toolkit III

An IDEAL VISION identifies and defines the kind of world we wish, with our partners, to create for tomorrow's child. It is ideal. The IDEAL VISION will help guide all organizational decisions and provide the rigorous basis for documenting the extent to which progress is being made. Two varieties of IDEAL VISIONS are provided in the Toolkit section: (1) a minimal IDEAL VISION devoid of MEANS, PROCESSES, philosophy, beliefs, and values; and (2) a consensus IDEAL VISION—provided in Toolkit IV—that includes consideration of beliefs, values, and philosophy. The use of the minimal IDEAL VISION is recommended because it does not lapse into MEANS and results below the MEGA level.

In the following chart, the first column contains the very basic elements of an IDEAL VISION. The second column contains some possible performance indicators for each. Please keep in mind that this is a minimal IDEAL VISION and has no philosophical content included.

Minimal Ideal Vision Element

Examples of Possible Performance Indicators

There will be no loss of human life or elimination of the survival of any species required for human survival. There will be no reductions in levels of self-sufficiency, quality of life, livelihood, or loss of property from any source including but not limited to the following:

As certified[1] by the Secretary General of the United Nations and verified as correct by the national Secretary of State within the last calendar year.

• war and/or riot

There will be no nonreversible, human-created changes as certified by the United Nations Secretary for the Environment, and no successful legal actions and findings as reported by the National Department of the Interior and/or documented and independently validated findings of irreversible environmental damage.

• unintended human-created change to the environment including the permanent destruction of the environment and/or rendering it nonrenewable

No species will go extinct from unintended human action as certified by the national department of health and/or the United Nations Secretary for the Environment.

• murder, rape, or crimes of violence, robbery, or destruction to person or property

There will be no murders, rapes, crimes of violence, robberies, or destruction to property as indicated by certified and audited reports of the chief law enforcement officer of the nation and/or those of each state and/or locality/region. These certified reports will be completed within the year.

---

[1]"As certified by" is to note that an official source is required to document and be accountable for the objectivity, validity, and reliability results-referenced data. For example, if an indicator is "as certified by the Secretary General of the United Nations" it could also be "or her/ his official designees."

- substance abuse

There will be no loss of life, or reduction in livelihood or quality of life from abusive use of controlled and uncontrolled substances as indicated by certified and audited reports of the chief national health officer, and/or state and/or local health and human services officer(s).

- disease and disability

There will be no loss of life, reduction in livelihood, quality of life from infectious diseases and associated disorder as indicated by certified and audited reports of the chief national health officer, and/or state and/or local health and human services officer(s).

- pollution

There will be no loss of life, or reduction in livelihood or quality of life from human produced pollutants and related toxic substances as indicated by certified and audited reports of the chief national health officer, and/or state and/or local health and human services officer(s) and/or the national chief health officer and/or the Secretary General of the United Nations.

- starvation and/or malnutrition

There will be no loss of life, or reduction in livelihood or quality of life from diagnosed starvation and/or malnutrition as indicated by certified and audited reports of the chief national health officer, and/or state and/or local health and human services officer(s).

- child abuse

There will be no loss of life, reduction in ability to function at or above the normative level for that individual, or reduction of quality of life from documented child abuse by other children and/or adults as indicated by certified and audited reports of the chief national health officer, and/or state and/or local health and human services officer(s), and/or law enforcement officer(s).

- partner/spouse abuse

There will be no loss of life, reduction in ability to function at or above the normative level for that individual, or reduction of quality of life from documented partner/spouse abuse by other children and/or adults as indicated by certified and audited reports of the chief national health officer, and/or state and/or local health and human services officer(s) and/or law enforcement officer(s).

- accidents, including transportation, home, and business/workplace

There will be no accidents in the home or residential dwelling, public and private transportation, or at and in the workplace that result in death, disability, loss or reduction of livelihood, reduction of quality of life as indicated by certified and audited reports of the national and/or international chief officer(s) for transportation and/or health and human services and/or law enforcement.

- discrimination based on irrelevant variables including color, race, creed, sex, religion, national origin, location

There will be no significant statistical difference (.05 level of confidence or beyond) among people on the basis of these variables as certified by the chief health and economic officer of the appropriate state or nation.

• poverty will not exist, and every woman and man will earn at least as much as it costs to live, unless he or she is progressing toward being self-sufficient and self-reliant.

No adult will be under the care, custody, or control of another person, agency, or substance. All adult citizens will be self-sufficient and self-reliant as certified in independently audited reports of the Secretary General of the United States, and/or national and/or state/regional chief officer for labor and employment security.

Key Enablers (not results at the MEGA level, but en route results that will likely be important in reaching MEGA level results):

• Any and all organizations—governmental, private sector/for-profit, public service/not-for-profit, educational—will contribute to the achievement and maintenance of this minimal IDEAL VISION and will be funded and continued to the extent to which it meets its objectives and that the minimum IDEAL VISION is accomplished and maintained.

• People will be responsible for what they use, do, and contribute and thus will not contribute to the reduction of any of the results identified in this minimal IDEAL VISION.

As indicated by certified and audited reports by the international and/or national and/or state/regional chief officer(s).

• no successful lawsuits and/or damage recovery related to any public or private organization.
• no public funding for any organization that does not document that it has contributed to no reduction or negative impact for any of the above elements in the IDEAL VISION as certified by an independent TaxWatch organization and/or other independent agency or agent.

No individual will be under the care, custody, or control of another person, agency, or substance, and his or her consumption will be equal to or less than their production as indicated by each having a positive credit rating and not being the recipient of government transfer payments other than social security. In addition, no person will be convicted of violating any law or policy related to each of the indicators of this minimal IDEAL VISION as certified by the appropriate officer(s) identified above.

ASSESSING YOUR IDEAL VISION

Completeness of the IDEAL VISION

It is often tempting to restrict the IDEAL VISION to one's own organization (or a client organization). It is difficult to set any direction for an organization if there is no relationship between what an organization does and delivers and the payoffs for external clients and society. Use your IDEAL VISION and sort each element into the Organizational Elements Model by identifying which of the elements it represents.

	MEGA/ OUTCOMES	MACRO/ OUTPUTS	MICRO/ PRODUCTS	PROCESSES	INPUTS
IDEAL VISION ELEMENT **1.** **2.** **3.**					

1. How many of the elements in the IDEAL VISION relate only to societal impact and consequences—MEGA/OUTCOMES level?

    Actions to take: If there are any elements that do not deal only with the MEGA/OUTCOMES level—societal impact and consequences—either eliminate them for now (they may be useful later in the strategic planning process) or ask, "If I accomplished this, what would the result be?" Keep asking this question until the element is eliminated or converted to a MEGA-level element that includes rigorous criteria.

2. How many of the elements in the IDEAL VISION relate only with MEANS, methods, or resources—the PROCESSES and/or INPUTS?

    Actions to take: If there are any elements that deal with MEANS, methods and/or resources, either eliminate them for now (they may be useful later in identifying and selecting methods and MEANS) or ask, "If I successfully used or did this, what would the result be?" Keep asking this question until the element is eliminated or converted to a MEGA-level element with measurable criteria.

3. How many of the elements in the IDEAL VISION make logic-leaps (moving from unwarranted assumptions to foregone conclusions) from a MEANS, method, belief, or value to the intended results? (For example, "Because all people are at peace with themselves and have good self-esteem, there will be no deaths from declared or undeclared war…".)

    Actions to take: If there are any logic-leaps, either eliminate them or ask, "If I eliminated this statement, what would the result be?" Keep asking this question until the element is eliminated or converted to a MEGA-level element with rigorous criteria that do not include beliefs, values, and/or approaches. Often, some item (such as one current organization or a favored approach) is so highly prized by an individual that she or he wants to classify it as MEGA even though it might be a Process or an Input. Recall that all of the Organizational Elements are equally important, and that they must be linked. Importance is not the same as MEGA.

4. A vital question to be asked about your IDEAL VISION is, "To what level am I willing to commit to strive for and get ever closer to achieving the vision?" Ask yourself the following:
    • What am I willing to risk to reach success? (Recall that there is no success without risk of failure and that failure often comes from not making a required and timely change.)
    • How hard am I willing to work to reach success?

5. What are the risks to me and my organization if I do not commit to constantly strive to achieve the IDEAL VISION?

The more you are willing to risk—sensible risk is where the results outweigh that which is given up—and the harder you are willing to work for success, then the more committed you are to your IDEAL VISION. You must be your own judge for this question. If you are not committed, then yours may not be an IDEAL VISION.

Using the Organizational Elements Model (OEM) as an Organizational Analysis Tool

The OEM may be used to calibrate what your organization uses, does, produces, and delivers, and the impact the OUTPUTS have. To identify what is missing and what is working in your organization, do the following:

1. Set up an OEM matrix.

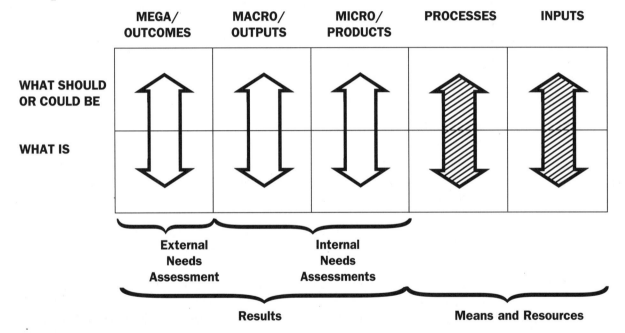

Figure 3.1 The Organizational Elements Model. Identified are the two levels of concern: What Should Be and What Is. Also identified are the three types of NEEDS and two types of QUASI-NEEDS. (34)

2. Fill in, for both the What Is and the What Should Be (or Could Be) dimensions, what your organization uses, does, produces, and delivers, and the payoffs and consequences.

3. Note the following:
    • empty cells indicating that there might be lapses in your organizational efforts, results, and contributions;
    • lack of firm linkages between cells in the OEM indicating that there might be lapses in the connections/linking among organizational efforts, results, and contributions;
    • lack of a What Should Be for one or more of the Organizational Elements that might indicate that what is being used, done, and delivered is not making a positive contribution to what the organization must deliver.

4. Identify what is working and what is not, and make revisions as required.
Applications of the OEM are also provided in Toolkit I.

Measurability of the IDEAL VISION

An IDEAL VISION should be stated in terms of precise and measurable indicators. These measurable indicators are used both for plotting your pathway—developing your strategic map—and for evaluating and continuously improving both your progress and your final accomplishments. Everything is measurable, at least on one of the four scales. (35, 52)

For each element of the IDEAL VISION statement, identify which of them is measurable on an interval or ratio scale. Because interval and ratio are more reliable measures, the more that can be measured at that level, the better. Make up a table, fill in the elements, and then check off the proper category (Nominal, Ordinal, Interval, Ratio) for each.

IDEAL VISION ELEMENT	Nominal	Ordinal	Interval	Ratio
Element 1				
Element 2				
Element 3				
etc.				

Actions to take. Total the number of elements in each of the various scales of measurement types (Nominal, Ordinal, Interval, Ratio). Then find the percentage for each type. The more reliable the measures and criteria, the greater confidence you may have in them. Interval and Ratio indicators provide you with the best basis for determining whether you have achieved your objectives (in fact, we define an objective as a result statement measurable on an Interval or Ratio scale.) They also provide the solid basis for evaluation and continuous improvement. The closer you are to 100 percent, the more confidence you may have in the usefulness of your IDEAL VISION and the precision of your resulting strategic planning and NEEDS ASSESSMENTs.

If 20 percent of the criteria are Nominal and/or Ordinal, that should alert you to a serious problem with the reliability of measurement. You should make all elements measurable on an Interval or Ratio scale. By limiting yourself to Nominal or Ordinal indicators, with a score of 50 percent or less, you risk confusion concerning what you are to achieve and when you have achieved the results you intended to deliver.

For each indicator that is in nominal- and ordinal-scale terms, ask, "How would I know when this was accomplished?" Often the unchallenged belief is that things are not measurable. If you can't name it, you don't know that it exists. Push for more reliability of measurement as you move from Nominal- and Ordinal- to Interval- and Ratio-scale indicators.

Toolkit IV

Ideal Visioning:
Practical Dreaming

An IDEAL VISION defines, in measurable performance terms, the kind of world we want for tomorrow's child. Basing all planning and doing on an IDEAL VISION is practical. You are defining the dream you can make come true. Starting with an IDEAL VISION is the safest starting point you can have for planning and doing. Organizations, all of them, are MEANS to societal ENDS. If an organization does not intend to make a positive contribution to its external clients and our shared society, it has no realistic future. Making money and doing good are not mutually exclusive. In fact, more and more organizational experts are insisting that doing societal good is no longer an organizational option, but a must. (10, 11, 12, 20, 21, 32, 35, 37, 38, 46, 49, 51) When using an IDEAL VISION, it is very important to note that it is the whole IDEAL VISION that is to be accomplished, not just one part or another. Consider the IDEAL VISION as a whole. An example of a minimal IDEAL VISION is presented in Toolkit III.

This Toolkit provides another version of an IDEAL VISION that includes people's initial beliefs, values, and philosophy. It is provided to show you what an IDEAL VISION might look like when a group of planners begins to build a consensus with people who are not yet comfortable with, or who have no experience with, precise and rigorous measurable criteria (Toolkit VI). The use of the minimal IDEAL VISION, however, is recommended.

A consensus IDEAL VISION

In Toolkit III you reviewed a minimal IDEAL VISION. That is not the only type of IDEAL VISION. Following is another variety, a consensus IDEAL VISION. It is an integration of IDEAL VISIONs that have been developed by organizations in every part of our world except for Central and South Africa and the former Soviet Union. Because it as an amalgam of what people identify as important, it contains some non–MEGA-level items. It does, however, capture what people tend to agree on for a definition of the kind of world they want for their grandchildren. The second type of IDEAL VISION is a "minimal IDEAL VISION," that is, one that has been stripped of the meanings superimposed by individual and group philosophies and values.

Here is an example of a consensus IDEAL VISION.

The people of the world will be at peace, and there will be no murder, rape, starvation, crime, or injurious substance abuse. Everyone will feel and be secure and move around their community, state, nation, and world safely and without regard to time or place. The world will be free of injurious and disabling disease as well as from disabling or death due to pollution, poisons, or other toxic substances introduced through human actions.

Every child brought into the world will be wanted. Poverty will not exist, and every person will earn at least as much as it costs to live, unless he or she is progressing toward being self-sufficient and self-reliant. No adult will be under the care, custody, or control of another person, agency, or substance.

All citizens will be encouraged to help themselves so that they become and stay self-sufficient and self-reliant and have a positive quality of life. People will take charge of their lives and be responsible for what they use, do, and contribute. Personal, intimate, and loving partnerships will form and sustain themselves.

No species will become extinct because of unintended human intervention or action. Beaches, cities, towns, and countrysides will be free of litter, graffiti, and defacement. There will be no accidents and, therefore, no accidental death, disability, or decrement in daily living.

The government's contribution will be to assist people to be happy and self-sustaining, and will reinforce independence and mutual contribution. It will be organized and funded to the extent to that it meets its objectives.

Viable business will earn a profit without bringing harm to its clients or the mutual world.

Here is an example of a consensus IDEAL VISION where rigorous (Interval and/or Ratio Scale) measurable criteria have been added.

The world will be at peace, with no loss of life or disability from declared or undeclared wars as certified by the United Nations and the US State Department.

There will be no murder, rape, crime, starvation or injurious substance abuse as certified by the Attorney General (AG), and/or Department of Health & Human Services (DH&HS.)

All people will feel and be secure and move around their city, state, nation, and the world safely, without regard to time or place as indicated by a zero rate of personal assaults as certified by the AG. There will be no admissions to prison, or requirements to imprison as certified by the US Department of Justice (USDJ). The recidivism rate for prisoners will be zero as certified by the USDJ.

The world will be free of injurious and disabling infectious disease as well as from disabling or death due to pollution, poison, or other toxic substances introduced through human actions, as certified by the DH&HS and/or the Centers for Disease Control.

The unlucky and unfortunate among us will be assisted to help themselves so that they will be increasingly close to being—and becoming—self-sufficient and self-reliant, as indicated by an increase in life expectancies for the population and an increase in the amount of money they produce and contribute so their consumption is at least equal to their production as certified by the US Department of Labor (USDL). Their quality of life will be such that there are no suicides or self-inflicted injuries, and they will rate their situation as acceptable or better, using a valid attitude instrument.

People will take charge of their lives, and be responsible for the consequences of their choices concerning what they use, do, and contribute as indicated by an absence of incarcerations, and of personal or physical abuse of others or of substances, and by 100 percent voter registration with voter turnout among them at least once every two years, as further certified by the AG and/or USDJ.

Personal, intimate, and loving partnerships will form and sustain themselves as indicated by a zero divorce rate, no judgments of physical abuse for persons living together, as certified by the DH&HS.

Every child brought into the world will be wanted, as indicated by no child's living below the poverty level, no child abuse, no starvation, etc. Each individual's consumption will be at least equal to or less than his or her production, as certified by the USDL. There will be zero convictions for child abuse as certified by the DH&HS. Poverty will not exist, and every person will earn at least as much as it costs to live unless he or she is moving toward being self-sufficient and self-reliant, as when going to school. No adult will be under the care, custody, or control of another person, agency, or substance as certified by the DH&HS and/or the USDL.

No species will go extinct from unintended human causes as certified by the Department of Environmental Resources. There will be no deaths or disabilities from accidents as certified by the Department of Transportation, and/or the National Safety Council.

The government's primary contribution will be to assist people to be happy and self-sustaining as well as to reinforce independence and mutual contribution. The government will be organized and funded to the extent that it meets its objectives as indicated by funding levels and MEGA-level results referenced by agency budgets and evaluations, as certified by an independent "TaxWatch" organization.

Viable business will earn a profit without bringing harm to its clients or the mutual world as certified by the US Departments of Commerce, Interior, and/or DH&HS.

Please note that the suggested minimal IDEAL VISION has been derived from consensus IDEAL VISIONs. Perceptions and views of an IDEAL VISION have been collected from around the world. Therefore, the minimal IDEAL VISION is based on an extensive collection of views of many diverse people.

Using an IDEAL VISION

In order for you to use an IDEAL VISION and get the most power from it, the following exercise might be useful.

Exercise 4.1

Using either a consensus or a minimal IDEAL VISION, derive an IDEAL VISION for use by either your organization or a client organization. (If you wish, you may prepare one yourself.) Keep these ground rules in mind.

1. An IDEAL VISION is ideal. It defines, in measurable performance terms, the kind of world you and your partners want for tomorrow's child.
2. Take the long view.
3. Dream. Be idealistic. Imagine a perfect world.
4. Don't worry if, at first, it doesn't seem achievable. You might not be able to get there in your lifetime or your children's, but at least you will know where you are headed. You can track your continuous progress.
5. Remember that you and your organization will not be responsible for achieving all of the IDEAL VISION, just a part of it.
6. Define ENDS to be accomplished, not MEANS (or resources). Make the ENDS, or objectives, measurable on an Interval or Ratio scale. This is the place not for poetry, but for measurable indicators of the kind of world you want for your grandchildren.
7. When writing objectives, including for the IDEAL VISION, use the "ABCD" format.
   - A(udience): recipients, target groups. Who benefits?
   - B(ehavior): performance, accomplishment, result. These are ENDS, not MEANS.
   - C(onditions): under what circumstances and in what environment will the performance/behavior be accomplished?
   - D(ata): criteria, ideally on an interval or ratio scale, that will be used to calibrate success. Data will show you how to tell when you have reached your desired ENDS.

Use Table 4.1 to develop your own IDEAL VISION. Remember to keep everything at the MEGA level, identify only ENDS, and never include any MEANS or resources to achieve the ENDS.

DESCRIBE THE WORLD IN WHICH YOU AND YOUR PARTNERS WANT TOMORROW'S CHILD TO LIVE AND ARE WILLING TO COOPERATIVELY ACHIEVE:
LIST THE CRITERIA (IN "ABCD" TERMS) TO BE USED TO DETERMINE YOUR PROGRESS AND SUCCESS:

Table 4.1 A format for creating an IDEAL VISION.

Toolkit V

A Strategic Planning Agreement Table.
Getting Commitment to MEGA-Level Thinking
and Planning: Helping Others See the
Importance of Linking Everything to
an IDEAL VISION

Starting all thinking, planning, and subsequent interventions and organizational development with links to the MEGA level represents a paradigm shift (2, 3, 4, 20) to many. In fact, some people get out of their comfort zones when asked to "think MEGA." Actually, doing so is the most practical and safe thing you can do. After all, if you and your organization do not intend to make a positive societal contribution, your future is limited. Table 5.1 provides a Strategic Planning Agreement Table that allows you and your organizational partners to face the basic questions and realities to be faced, note the linkages between planning and results at the various levels, and choose to buy into or out of the decision to use the consequent results chain. Most people, when reviewing the questions in the Agreement Table, realize that this approach is sensible, rational, and practical.

Using the Agreement Table should assist you and others to realize the importance of linking MEGA, MACRO, and MICRO levels of planning and results to what the organization uses, does, produces, and delivers. This can be a powerful process for getting everyone committed to MEGA-level planning and thinking. By "walking through" these questions, most people quickly realize the importance of MEGA-level strategic thinking and planning.

	Response			
	Client		Planners	
Strategic Thinking and Planning Agreement Factors	Y	N	Y	N
1. The total organization, as well as each facility, will contribute to the client's and society's survival, health, and well-being.				
2. The total organization, as well as each facility, will contribute to the client's and society's quality of life.				
3. Client's and society's survival, health, and well-being will be part of the mission objectives for the organization and each of its facilities.				
4. Each organizational operational function will have objectives that contribute to #1, #2, and #3.				
5. Each job/task will have objectives that contribute to #1, #2, and #3.				
6. A NEEDS ASSESSMENT will identify and document any gaps in results at the operational levels of #1, #2, #3, #4, and #5.				
7. Human resources/training and/or operations requirements will be generated from the NEEDS identified and selected based on the results of #6.				
8. The results of #6 may recommend non-HRD/training interventions.				
9. Evaluation and Continuous Improvement will compare results with objectives for #1, #2, #3, #4, and 5.				

Table 5.1 A Strategic Thinking and Planning Agreement Table. (34, 35, 38, 40)

Toolkit VI

Making Your Objectives Rigorous and Precise

Some people don't care for measurable objectives. They either are concerned that making things measurable will only capture the trivial or that there are just some things that are not measurable. Neither one of these should be an issue if you are careful and caring.

Confusing "measurable" with "trivial" can happen, but only if you let it. Make certain that the objectives cover everything that is important. The Organizational Elements Model (OEM) will identify the necessary and related areas for which measurable objectives should exist.

Now for the concerns that there might be some things that are not measurable. We might not often think of measurability in quite these terms, but note that if you can name it, you are measuring it. Even by saying that some things are not measurable, you are making two piles: measurable things and nonmeasurable things. In fact, naming is the least reliable level of measurement—but a measurement all the same—called Nominal-scale measurement.

Scale of Measurement	Type of Result
Nominal	names, labels
Ordinal	ranks
Interval	equal scale distances with arbitrary zero-point
Ratio	equal scale distances with known zero-point

Table 6.1 A taxonomy of results. (34, 52)

Here is another aid to better ensure that your objectives are precise and rigorous, the "Hey, Mommy Test."[1] Use it to help prepare measurable objectives and ensure that they are reasonable. When preparing a statement of results, subject it to the scenario of a child coming to Mother and saying, "Hey, Mommy, let me show you how I can (and fill in the would-be objective)." If it targets a result, it will be obvious. For example, how does this sound: "Hey, Mommy, let me show you that I have a deep and profound love of learning." Without any performance specifications, this doesn't make much sense, does it? Now try this one: "Hey, Mommy, let me show you that I have a deep and profound commitment to total quality because of the number of Pareto Diagrams I draw each week." Make certain that all MEGA-level objectives (and the MACRO and MICRO ones as well) pass the "ABCD"[2] test or Mager's format for objectives. (42)

---

[1] I originally attributed this to Bob Mager, but he tells me that this wasn't his. It is the kind of insightful tool that I associate with his clear thinking and work.

[2] I do not know who originated this concept. I have, however, modified this over time.

A Format for Preparing Measurable Objectives:
As Easy as **ABCD**

A: Who or what is the **A**udience, target, or recipient?

B: What **B**ehavior, performance, accomplishment, end, consequence, or result is to be demonstrated?

C: Under what **C**onditions will the behavior or accomplishment be observed?

D: What **D**ata—criteria, ideally measured on an interval or ratio scale—will be used to calibrate success?

Figure 6.1 An ABCD format for preparing useful objectives. (35, 39)

Also useful and well accepted is the Mager-type objective (42) format that identifies the following:
- what is to be accomplished,
- who or what will demonstrate the accomplishment,
- under what conditions the accomplishment will be observed, and
- what criteria (ideally on an Interval or Ratio scale) will be used to indicate success.

Precise statements of intended results allow you to determine where you are headed, define how you will know when you have arrived, plot your progress toward your destination, and identify what has to be changed and what to be maintained to get from where you are to where you wish to be.

There are a number of steps you can take to ensure that your objectives are both measurable and useful.

Checking the completeness and appropriateness of your objectives

Figure 6.2 provides a series of templates, or guidelines, to assure that your performance indicators
- address ENDS, not MEANS,
- are measurable in rigorous terms so there is no confusion over whether or not you delivered,
- address important organizational issues, and
- consider both current results and desired ones.

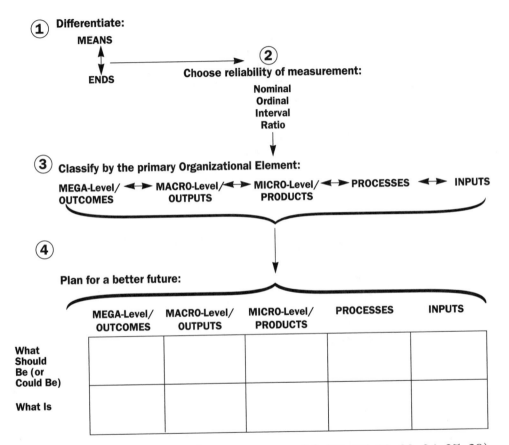

Figure 6.2 A template for ensuring that your objectives are useful. (26, 27, 28, 29, 34, 35, 39)

Here is the rationale for each "template" in Figure 6.2.

1. ENDS/MEANS. The first template asks you to assure that your indicators target ENDS—results, payoffs, consequences, performance—not MEANS (such as training, teaching, developing).

2. Reliability of measurement. The four scales of measurement as shown in Table 6.1 are
   - naming (Nominal);
   - rank ordering (Ordinal);
   - relative scaling with equal scale distances and an arbitrary zero point, like reporting the outside temperature or reporting standard deviations on tests (Interval);
   - absolute scaling with equal scale distances where there are equal scale distances and a known and fixed zero point like temperature in Kelvin, weight, distance (Ratio).

When you write useful indicators, the more reliable the criteria—the more rigorous and precise—the more confidence you may have in what they target and what they will deliver. All of your indicators should be measurable on an Interval or Ratio scale.

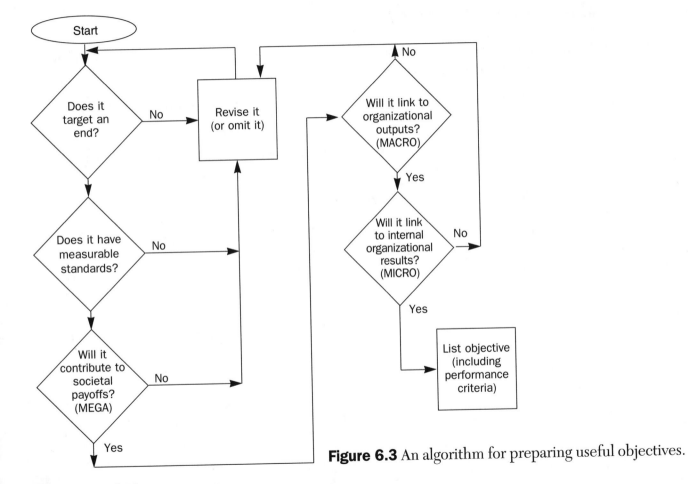

Figure 6.3 An algorithm for preparing useful objectives.

3. Classification by the primary organizational element. After going through the "filter" of #1 and #2 you should check to make certain that the indicator targets an END (MEGA/OUTCOMES, MACRO/OUTPUTS, or MICRO/PRODUCTS.) If it targets a PROCESS (a MEANS) or an INPUT (resources, ingredients), then there has been a breakdown at Step #1 and revision or elimination of the indicator is required. The OEM allows you to identify an indicator as a MEANS or an END, and at what level of result it is.

4. Plan for a better future. Next you can ensure that the indicator has both a What Should Be (or Could Be) and a What Is set of dimensions to it. If there is only a What Is indicator without a What Should Be (or Could Be) companion, you are probably not identifying a future set of results and consequences.

Using all four templates allows you not only to ensure that your indicators focus on precise, rigorous ENDS—measures on a Interval or Ratio scale—but also lets you know that you are relating to MEGA/OUTCOMES as well. In addition, you may ensure that your indicator also identifies a What Should Be (or Could Be) dimension so you may help create a better future.

Toolkit VII

Level and Scope of Strategic Thinking and the Related Mission Objective

<table>
<tr><td>

**Toolkit
VII**

</td><td>

To help ensure that you have the most useful level of strategic thinking and planning and the associated MISSION OBJECTIVE, the following can be useful. Here is a process for calibrating your strategic plan to ascertain if it really is strategic.

</td></tr>
</table>

Exercise 7.1

Is the strategic plan you are using (or creating) appropriate and as powerful as possible? Review it and answer the following questions.

1. What level of primary focus was selected for the strategic plan?
   a. MEGA/Societal
   b. MACRO/Organizational
   c. MICRO/Individual or small group
   d. PROCESSES, methods, activities, interventions
   e. Resources, INPUTS
2. Take the mission statement (or better, the MISSION OBJECTIVE[1] you derived for your strategic plan) and determine, for each element, which ones deal with MEGA, MACRO, MICRO (or, inappropriately, with MEANS and/or resources.)

---

[1]A MISSION OBJECTIVE states in measurable terms both where you are headed and what criteria on an Interval or Ratio scale will be used to measure success. A mission statement only identifies where you are headed.

Use the following job aid to conduct this analysis. Place elements in the IDEAL VISION you have selected to form your MISSION OBJECTIVE (MACRO level) into the appropriate columns, MEGA/OUTCOMES, MACRO/OUTPUTS, MICRO/PRODUCTS.

IDEAL ELEMENT SELECTED FOR MISSION OBJECTIVE	MEGA/ OUTCOMES-RELATED	MACRO/ OUTPUTS-RELATED	MICRO/ PRODUCTS-RELATED
ELEMENT 1			
ELEMENT 2			
ELEMENT 3			
ELEMENT N			

Determining the level of your MISSION OBJECTIVE

Analyze the MISSION OBJECTIVE—the MACRO level—and identify the number of elements that are derived from the MEGA/OUTCOMES from the IDEAL VISION. Remember that the MISSION OBJECTIVE includes the MEGA/OUTCOME level indicators that your organization has committed to deliver—either by itself or in cooperation with other agencies or agents. Pay close attention to the performance indicators, or criteria used. Identify who really is to be the primary client and beneficiary of what the MISSION OBJECTIVE and the resulting plan will deliver.

MEGA: When the primary client and beneficiary of the strategic plan is (or will be) society and the community—now and in the future—as identified in the IDEAL VISION, and when there are performance indicators included in the MISSION OBJECTIVE that identify such (e.g., no murders; all graduates and completers employed at or above subsistence level for at least six months; no deaths or disabilities from organizationally generated pollutants, etc.), the plan is MEGA-level referenced.

MACRO: When the MISSION OBJECTIVE and performance indicators are targeted at organizational contributions alone (automobiles delivered, sales, services completed and billed, etc.)[2] and not linked to selected elements identified in the IDEAL VISION, the plan is restricted to the MACRO level because there are no links to the MEGA level or the IDEAL VISION.

MICRO: When the MISSION OBJECTIVE and performance indicators intend to achieve results for individuals or small groups (fenders completed, customers billed, etc.), it is at the MICRO level because there are no formal links to the MEGA or MACRO level.

PROCESSES and INPUTS: When the plan addresses methods and MEANS (contact hours, time on computers, hours committed to writing, etc.,) the plan is PROCESS-related. When the plan focuses on resources (number of computers, number of learners per classroom, teacher credential levels, class size) it is INPUT/resources-related.

---

[2] For example, seeking only "92 percent on-time delivery to external clients" without also requiring that what we deliver will contribute to their safety, quality of life, and the environment (as one instance of societal-contribution) will not necessarily contribute to getting ever closer to the Ideal Vision.

Actions to take: If the scope of your MISSION OBJECTIVE, as we urge, is all MEGA—it relates and will contribute to the achievement of the IDEAL VISION—your MISSION OBJECTIVE is excellent and appropriate. If your selected scope is some MEGA with mostly MACRO, give yourself the opportunity to improve your success by converting all of the elements of the MISSION OBJECTIVE to the MEGA/OUTCOMES level. If your scope is MICRO, give yourself credit for at least being results-oriented and convert all to the MEGA/OUTCOMES level. If your scope is PROCESSES and/or resources, realize that you are not likely to be successful. A results orientation is vital, and a MEGA focus is critical. To the extent that your planning remains results-oriented and keeps the IDEAL VISION in mind, you can attain maximum success.

Remove (or hold until later in the planning process) any elements that are focused on MEANS and not ENDS and any that are not directly related to the IDEAL VISION. When system planning continues to identify building-block functions—those PRODUCTS that, when combined, will achieve the mission—then the lower level objectives will be useful if they contribute to the accomplishment of the mission and contribute toward the accomplishment of the IDEAL VISION.

Toolkit VIII

Estimating Your Return on Investment: Comparing What You Give With What You Get

<table>
<tr><td>

Toolkit VIII

</td><td>

If not now, soon you will be required to justify everything you use, spend, and deliver on the basis of the costs to you and the consequences of what you deliver. You can no longer just spend and hope for the best. You have to show what you get for what you give. You have to be accountable for both your results and the payback for them.

</td></tr>
</table>

It is virtually impossible to take into account all of the possible costs and the various kinds of consequences, but you can estimate them closely enough to justify what you do and deliver, and to track your costs and returns. This book strongly urges you to base all strategic planning and thinking on the MEGA level by considering what the payoffs and consequences are for your external clients and our shared world.

An indicator of MEGA-level consequences for individuals

One way to estimate the societal impact—MEGA-level consequences, or a cost-utility payoff—is that an individual's consumption should be equal to or less than his or her production. (31, 34)

$$C \leq P$$

where C is consumption as indicated by dollars/money expended by an individual and
P is production as indicated by dollars/money obtained by an individual.

This indicator—an approximation of MEGA-level consequences and payoffs—is only for an individual, and uses money as a proxy for costs and consequences. A basic definition for MEGA-level results is that no person will be under the care, custody, or control of another person, agency, or substance, and that is also indicated by $C \leq P$.

Using costs-consequences analyses to estimate a full return on investment: An example using a human resources development (HRD)/performance technology department

Economists, by and large, prefer a full analysis of all input costs and all consequences, as shown in column 1 of Table 8.1. This column identifies possible variables for an HRD/performance technology department in any organization. (30) When such data do not exist or cannot be obtained in time for a decision, then some of the variables for a proper return on investment may be used to approximate a full study. Such critical items for an HRD department used as an example are noted in Table 8.1 with a shaded box. Columns 2 and 3 in Table 8.1 identify whether a variable relates to "costs" or to "consequences."

POSSIBLE VARIABLES	RELATED TO COSTS	RELATED TO CONSEQUENCES	CURRENT RESULTS/ STATUS	DESIRED RESULTS/ STATUS
Current expenditures	X			
Opportunity costs	X			
Societal "spin-offs"		X		
Current departmental budget	X			
Costs of interventions (training, Continuous Improvement, etc.) a. Salaries and related benefits b. Facilities c. Equipment d. Expenses	X X			
Costs to attend or participate in intervention a. Contributions by participant b. Contributions by others (e.g. employers, other funds, etc.) c. Opportunity costs				

POSSIBLE VARIABLES	RELATED TO COSTS	RELATED TO CONSEQUENCES	CURRENT RESULTS/ STATUS	DESIRED RESULTS/ STATUS
Change (reduction or increase) in revenue and/or expenditures		X		
Change in productivity of employees		X		
Increase in employee morale		X		
Drop-out/completion rates		X		
Change in expenditures of participants (include opportunity costs)		X		
Participants enrolled simultaneous programs	X			
Etc.				

Table 8.1 Approximating a full return on investment analysis: A Costs-Consequences Analysis.

For each variable, the analysis should identify the gap between current results and status (column 4 in Table 8.1) and required or desired results (column 5 in Table 2). It should be noted that other interventions and different organizational missions would use a unique and distinctive set of return on investment and costs-consequences variables. Therefore, there would be different variables identified for a Costs-Consequences Analysis. Consequently, a NEEDS ASSESSMENT—determination of gaps between current and desired results—is performed on each of the variables to determine what is working and what might not be effective.

The shaded items are the minimum that should be included in a Costs-Consequences Analysis to provide a coarse-grained identification of the current or anticipated merit of a program, project, or intervention. All the variables would be required of a conventional return on investment analysis.

Listed below are the questions a costs-consequences initiative should answer.
1. Who are the participants in the interventions? Who should be?
2. Who is being turned down for the interventions? Who should be?
3. What interventions are the participants getting? What alternative interventions might they get?
4. What are the results of the intervention or interventions (at the MEGA, MACRO, and MICRO levels)?
5. What are the completion, drop-out, and continuation rates for the participants?
6. What are the performance levels of the completers? Of the leavers and the noncompleters?
7. What is the societal condition—the levels of self-sufficiency, self-reliance, and quality of life—of the completers? The noncompleters? What are the levels of completers' and noncompleters' self-sufficiency and self-reliance in terms at least of $C \leq P$?
8. What interventions and patterns of interventions are making the best contributions in terms of societal (MEGA) payoffs and consequences? What is working and what is not? What are the valid criteria for these?
9. What are the societal (MEGA) payoffs and consequences for the various interventions for the various kinds of participants in terms at least of $C \leq P$?
10. What are the costs for the payoffs and nonpayoffs? Are the expenditures worthwhile as compared to other interventions that might be made?

11. Have the decisions made not generalized past the completeness and quality of the data?

Using Costs-Consequences Analysis in any organization

Keeping in mind the Organizational Elements Model and the concept of costs-consequences, the following questions allow for the identification of what was missing in order for useful Evaluation and Continuous Improvement to occur:
1. What data exist?
2. What data do not exist?
3. What are critical data required by the project/intervention to determine effectiveness, efficiency, and positive costs-consequences?
4. What Organizational Elements data exist?
5. What Organizational Elements data are missing complete and valid data?
6. Are the gaps between What Is and What Should Be identified?
7. Are all of the Organizational Elements linked? (Does a "flow" from element to element exist, and is it justified?)

Evaluation, Continuous Improvement, and Quality Management

Evaluation is the process of comparing objectives with accomplishments, and identifying what was successful with what was not. Unfortunately, evaluation data are often used for blaming and not for fixing. The process of Continuous Improvement (sometimes called Total Quality Management) intends to change our ways of doing things from simply evaluating our results to using data to improve our processes and thus our contributions. (8, 17, 18, 32, 37, 39)

Objectives, as discussed in Toolkit VI, are vital. As Bob Mager pointed out so many years ago, if you don't know where you are headed, you might end up someplace else. Also important is to find out if you are making progress—Continuous Improvement—toward useful objectives; in other words, moving up the results chain from MEANS to ENDS as shown in Toolkit II. Human resource development and performance technology specialists spend much of their time on training, only one intervention among many possibilities. Much attention has been given to evaluating training, but few trainers have allowed a professional to check to make certain that Continuous Improvement is being made—improvement not only in MICRO products (mastery of training content), but also in what organizations deliver to external clients (MACRO), and in the external client and societal (MEGA) payoffs.

Evaluation Levels
MEGA level 5. Societal consequences: societal and client responsiveness, contributions, usefulness, and payoffs.
MACRO level 4. Organizational results: organizational contributions.
MICRO level 3. Successful application: individual and small-group utilization within the organization. 2. Acquisition: individual and small-group mastery and competence.
PROCESS 1b. Reactions: method-means and processes' acceptability and efficiency.
INPUT 1a. Enabling: availability and quality of human, financial, and physical resources.

Table 8.2 Five levels of evaluation of human performance improvement interventions. (based on 30)

An extension of Kirkpatrick's four-level evaluation process (40) has been provided by Kaufman & Keller so that the links between organizational contributions and external contributions may be identified.

When examining the results and contributions of any intervention, this extension of Kirkpatrick's training evaluation process can help assure you that not only did you meet your organizational objectives but you also ensured that it was making a MEGA-level contribution. And making a MEGA-level contribution is also a key element in the demonstration of positive costs-consequences delivering results that were useful both inside and outside the organization.

Toolkit IX

Quality Management Plus

Quality Management Plus (QM+) (25, 32 , 34, 35, 37, 39) adds the MEGA level to conventional Total Quality Management (TQM). Doing so avoids having a very successful quality program that delivers OUTPUTS to clients and society that are not useful. Scrutinizing and deeply questioning your organizational purposes and initiatives is basically rational and vital. (1, 3, 5 ,6, 7, 11 ,13, 14, 15, 16 , 24, 34, 43, 44, 45, 46, 47, 48, 49, 50, 51, 53, 54) You cannot solve today's problems with the same thinking and PARADIGMS that create them.

Figure 9.1 shows the elements of both conventional Quality Management (shaded boxes) and the additional functions required to make it complete and responsive by including the MEGA level (plain boxes) in the Quality Management process.

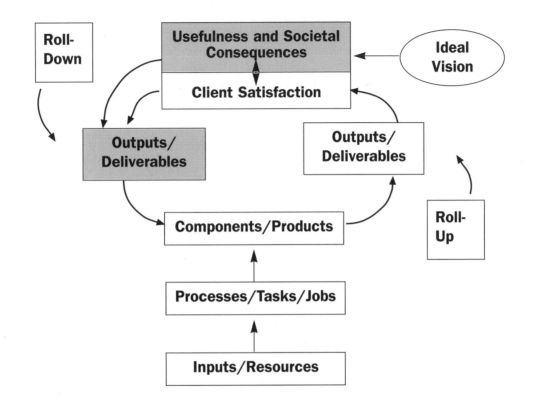

The Total Quality Management Plus cycle. Conventional Total Quality Management (TQM) elements are shaded.

Figure 9.1 Relating conventional Quality Management with MEGA-level thinking.

To help Quality Management make the holistic contribution it can and should, here are some guidelines to help you integrate its application with strategic thinking and planning.

Exercise 9.1

1. Using the TQM/Continuous Improvement process and results your organization uses, what are the similarities and differences between your process and Quality Management Plus (QM+)?

2. What are the practical costs-consequences reasons for adding the MEGA level to existing TQM processes?

3. How would you explain to an associate or external client that you can save them time and money by using QM+?

4. Why is it cost effective to integrate the teams that are doing
    • TQM,
    • strategic planning,
    • NEEDS ASSESSMENT?

5. What are the relationships between Continuous Improvement and formative evaluation?

6. What are the relationships among conventional TQM, benchmarking, and reengineering?

7. What might be accomplished by adding the MEGA level to benchmarking and reengineering?

Toolkit X

Strategic Planning Plus

Toolkit X

Figure 10.1 is an algorithm for Strategic Planning Plus that you may use to determine whether your strategic plan has the basic elements to make it useful. Because there are three levels of results, there can be three starting places for planning. However, only the MEGA-level starting place delivers Strategic Planning Plus.

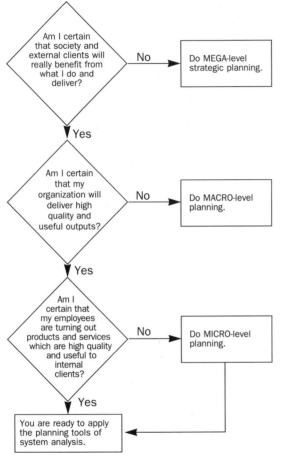

Figure 10.1 Questions involved in selecting a planning (or, best Strategic Planning Plus) level. (based on 34)

To help ensure that your strategic thinking and planing are useful, here is an exercise to consider.

Exercise 10.1

1. Compare your strategic plan with the steps in the algorithm and determine if it is MEGA, MACRO, or MICRO level. (It might be that it is none of the above.)

Note: A way to determine if it is MEGA (societal) focused is to determine if the elements of an IDEAL VISION (see exercise 4.1 in Toolkit IV) are included.

2. What are the implications for your internal and external clients' success with the plan you brought or with which you have worked?

3. If the strategic plan is not MEGA level, what will it take to modify it?

4. What are the penalties and payoffs for you and your internal and external clients for using a MEGA-level strategic plan?

5. Why do you think most strategic planning models and frameworks don't get to the MEGA level?

Toolkit XI

Summary Concepts

Six Critical Success Factors for Strategic Thinking and Planning

1. Move out of your comfort zones—today's PARADIGMS—and use newer, wider boundaries for thinking, planning, doing, and Continuous Improvement/Evaluation.

2. Define NEED as a gap in results (not as insufficient levels of resources, MEANS, or methods.) NEED is a noun, not a verb.

3. Differentiate between ENDS (what) and MEANS (how).

4. Use and relate all three levels of planning and results—MEGA/OUTCOMES, MACRO/OUTPUTS, MICRO/PRODUCTS.

5. Use an IDEAL VISION (what kind of world, in measurable performance terms, we want for tomorrow's child) as the underlying basis for all thinking, planning, doing, and Continuous Improvement.

6. All OBJECTIVES—including MISSION OBJECTIVES—should specify precise statements of both where you are headed and the exact criteria for measuring when you have arrived.

IDEAL VISIONS

1. Identify the future world we, and our societal partners, want to create together. It is not written for one's organization.

2. The IDEAL VISION is a statement, in measurable terms, of what kind of world we want for tomorrow's child. Using one is the safest and most practical and pragmatic starting place for planning and organizational improvement. If you and your organization are not moving ever closer to the IDEAL VISION, it is likely a solution to no known problem.
3. The MISSION OBJECTIVE for an organization identifies the elements of the IDEAL VISION the organization commits to deliver either alone or in partnership with others.

NEEDS and NEEDS ASSESSMENT

1. When you define a NEED as a gap between current and desired/required results, it gives you a three-way payoff:
   - It provides the criteria for planning.
   - It provides the criteria for Evaluation and Continuous Improvement.
   - It allows you to justify your budgets on the basis of what it costs to meet the NEED versus the costs to ignore it.

2. A NEEDS assessment identifies the gaps between current results and desired/required ones and places the NEEDS in priority order on the basis of "what it costs to meet the NEED" versus "what it costs to ignore the NEED."

Strategic Planning Plus

1. Strategic Planning Plus identifies where you and your organization should be headed, and identifies the building-block results required to get from here to there. It has three phases: (a) scoping, (b) planning, and (c) implementation and Evaluation/Continuous Improvement. It best starts with an IDEAL VISION.

2. Tactical planning identifies the alternative ways and MEANS to get the strategic plan accomplished. Operational planning identifies what must be done to implement the tactical plan successfully. Strategic planning, to obtain the most benefit, best starts with an IDEAL VISION.

3. Using a MEGA level as the starting place for the IDEAL VISION requires a shift in most current planning PARADIGMS. Do it. You cannot solve today's problems with the strategies, tools, and PARADIGMS that caused them.

4. The MEGA level is what is almost always missing from conventional approaches to strategic planning, NEEDS ASSESSMENT, reengineering, and Quality Management. It is the "plus" in Strategic Planning Plus, Quality Management Plus, benchmarking plus, and reengineering plus.

5. Leaders focus on the MEGA level, executives on the MACRO Level, and managers on the MICRO level.

The Organizational Elements Model (OEM)

1. The OEM identifies the elements characterizing every organization—OUTCOMES: the impact and payoffs of OUTPUTS in and for society; OUTPUTS: the results that can be delivered outside of the organization; PRODUCTS: building-block results that alone will not deliver organizational success;

PROCESSES: methods, how-to-do-its, activities; INPUTS: ingredients, starting conditions. INPUTS and PROCESSES identify MEANS, while PRODUCTS, OUTPUTS, and OUTCOMES are three related types of results.

2. The OEM may be arrayed in two levels, What Should Be and What Is. Because there are three types of results, there are three types of NEEDS.

3. The linkages between the organizational elements are vital to ensure that what an organization uses, does, produces, and delivers makes a positive contribution to external clients and society. The three levels of results—OUTCOMES, OUTPUTS, and PRODUCTS—form a results chain.

4. The OEM may be used for an organizational analysis. By sorting what is used, done, produced, delivered, and the external impact into the OEM, you may find out what is present, what is missing, and where links might be being omitted.

References and Related Readings

1. Argyris, C. (1991: May/June) "Teaching Smart People to Learn," *Harvard Business Review.'*

2. Barker, J.A. (1989) *The Business of Paradigms: Discovering the Future.* Videotape. Burnsville, MN: ChartHouse Learning Corp.

3. —. (1992) *Future Edge: Discovering the New Paradigms of Success.* New York: Morrow.

4. —. (1992) *Paradigm Pioneers. Discovering the Future Series.* Videotape. Burnsville, MN: ChartHouse Learning Corp.

5. Block, P. (1993) *Stewardship.* San Francisco: Berrett-Koehler.

6. Carnevale, A.P. (1991) *America and the New Economy: How New Competitive Standards Are Radically Changing the American Workplace.* San Francisco: Jossey-Bass.

7. Conner, D.R. (1992) *Managing at the Speed of Change.* New York: Villard Books.

8. Crosby, P.B. (1992) *Quality Is Free: The Art of Making Quality Certain.* New York: McGraw-Hill.

9. Deal, T., & Kennedy, A. (1982) *Corporate Cultures: The Rites and Rituals of Corporate Life.* Reading, MA: Addison-Wesley.

10. Drucker, P.F. (1993) *Post-Capitalist Society.* New York: Harper Business.

11. —. (1994: November) "The Age of Social Transformation," *Atlantic Monthly,* pp. 53–80.

12. —. (1995: February) "Really Reinventing Government," *The Atlantic Monthly,* pp. 49–61.

13. Garratt, B., (Ed.) (1995) *Developing Strategic Thought: Rediscovering the Art of Direction-Giving.* London: McGraw-Hill.

14. Hamel, G., & Prahalad, C.K. (1994) *Competing for the Future: Breakthrough Strategies for Seizing Control of Your Industry and Creating the Markets of Tomorrow.* Boston: Harvard Business School Press.

15. Hammer, M., & Stanton, S.A. (1995) *The Reengineering Revolution: A Handbook.* New York: HarperCollins.

16. Howard, P.K. (1994) *The Death of Common Sense: How Law Is Suffocating America.* New York: Random House.

17. Joiner, B.L. (1986: May) "Using Statisticians to Help Transform Industry in America," *Quality Progress,* pp. 46–50.

18. Juran, J.M. (1988) *Juran on Planning for Quality.* New York: Free Press.

19. Kaufman, R. (1992: May) "Six Steps to Strategic Success," *Training & Development,* pp. 107–112.

20. —. (1992: July) "Comfort and Change: Natural Enemies," *Educational Technology.*

21. —. (1993: October) "Mega Planning: The Argument Is Over," *Performance & Instruction.*

22. —. (1994: February) "A Needs Assessment Audit," *Performance & Instruction.*

23. —. (1994: February) "Auditing Your Needs Assessment," *Training & Development*, pp. 22–23.

24. —. (1995: February) "Is Market-Driven Good Enough?" *Performance & Instruction*.

25. —. (1995: May/June) "Quality Management Plus: Beyond Standard Approaches to Quality," *Educational Technology*.

26. Kaufman, R., Grise, P., & Watters, K. (1992) "Selecting and Getting Agreement on the Scope of Needs Assessment and/or Strategic Planning." In K.L. Medsker and D.G. Roberts (Eds.), *ASTD Trainer's Toolkit: Evaluating the Results of Training*, p. 84. Alexandria, VA: The American Society for Training and Development.

27. Kaufman, R., Grise, P. & Watters, K. (1992) "Preparing Useful Performance Indicators." In K.L. Medsker and D.G. Roberts (eds.), *ASTD Trainer's Toolkit: Evaluating the Results of Training*, p. 88. Alexandria, VA: The American Society for Training and Development.

28. Kaufman, R., Grise, P., & Watters, K. (1992) "Are Our 'Needs' Needs and Are They Important?" In K.L. Medsker and D.G. Roverts (Eds.), *ASTD Trainer's Toolkit: Evaluating the Results of Training*, p. 90. Alexandria, VA: The American Society for Training and Development.

29. Kaufman, R., Grise, P., & Watters, K. (1992) "Needs Assessment Summary Forms," In K.L. Medsker and D.G Roberts (Eds.), *ASTD Trainer's Toolkit: Evaluating the Results of Training*, p. 92. Alexandria, VA: The American Society for Training and Development.

30. Kaufman, R., & Keller, J. (1994: Winter) "Levels of Evaluation: Beyond Kirkpatrick." *Human Resources Development Quarterly*, Vol. 5, No. 4.

31. Kaufman, R., & Watkins, R. (1996) "Costs-Consequences Analysis." *Human Resources Development Quarterly*.

32. Kaufman, R., & Swart, W. (1995: May/June) "Beyond Conventional Benchmarking: Integrating Ideal Visions, Strategic Planning, Reengineering, and Quality Management," *Educational Technology*.

33. Kaufman, R. (1988) *Identifying and Solving Problems: A Management Approach* (4th Ed.). Edgecliff, NSW, Australia: Social Impacts.

34. Kaufman, R. (1192) *Strategic Planning Plus: An Organizational Guide* (Revised Ed.). Newbury Park, CA: Sage.

35. Kaufman, R. (1995) *Mapping Educational Success* (Revised Ed.). Thousand Oaks, CA: Corwin Press.

36. Kaufman, R., Rojas, A.M., & Mayer, H. (1993) *Needs Assessment: A User's Guide*. Englewood Cliffs, NJ: Educational Technology.

37. Kaufman, R., & Zahn, D. (1993) *Quality Management Plus: The Continuous Improvement of Education*. Newbury Park, CA: Corwin Press.

38. Kaufman, R., & Grise, P. (1995) *How to "Audit" Your Strategic Plan: Making Good Education Better*. Thousand Oaks, CA: Corwin Press.

39. Kaufman, R., Herman, J., & Watters, K. (1996) *Educational Planning: Strategic, Tactical, Operational.* Lancaster, PA: Technomic Publishing Co.

40. Kirkpatrick, D. (1987) "Evaluation." In R.L. Craig, *Training & Development Handbook,* (3rd Ed.), pp. 301–319. New York: McGraw-Hill.

41. Kuhn, T. (1970) *The Structure of Scientific Revolutions* (2nd Ed.). Chicago: University of Chicago Press.

42. Mager, R.F. (1975) *Preparing Instructional Objectives* (2nd Ed.). Belmont, CA: Pitman Learning.

43. Marshall, R., & Tucker, M. (1992) *Thinking for a Living: Education and the Wealth of Nations.* New York: Basic Books.

44. Martin, R. (1993: November/December) "Changing the Mind of the Organization," *Harvard Business Review.*

45. Mitroff, I.I., Mason, R.O., & Pearson, C.M. (1994) "Radical Surgery: What Will Tomorrow's Organizations Look Like?" *Academy of Management Executives,* Vol. 8, No. 2.

46. Naisbitt, J., & Aburdene, P. (1990) *Megatrends 2000: Ten New Directions for the 1990s.* New York: Morrow.

47. Nanus, B. (1992) *Visionary Leadership.* San Francisco: Jossey-Bass.

48. Osborne, D, and Gaebler, T. (1992) *Reinventing Government: How the Entrepreneurial Spirit Is Transforming the Public Sector.* Reading, MA: Addison-Wesley.

49. Popcorn, F. (1991) *The Popcorn Report.* New York: Doubleday.

50. Rummler, G.A., & Brache A.P. (1990) *Improving Performance: How to Manage the White Space on the Organization Chart.* San Francisco: Jossey-Bass.

51. Senge, P.M. (1990) *The Fifth Discipline: The Art & Practice of the Learning Organization.* New York: Doubleday-Currency.

52. Stevens, S.S. (1951) "Mathematics, Measurement, and Psychophysics," *Handbook of Experimental Psychology.* New York: Wiley.

53. Toffler, A. (1990) *Powershift: Knowledge, Wealth, and Violence at the Edge of the 21st Century.* New York: Bantam.

54. Wheatley, M.J. (1992) *Leadership and the New Science: Learning About Organization From an Orderly Universe.* San Francisco: Berrett-Koehler.

55. Witkin, B.R. (1994) "Needs Assessment Since 1981: The State of Practice," *Evaluation Practice,* Vol. 15(1), pp. 17–27.

RELATED READINGS

Anderson, L.G., & Settle, R.F. (1977) *Benefit-Cost Analysis: A Practical Guide.* Lexington, MA: Lexington Books.

Blanchard, K., & Peale, N.V. (1988) *The Power of Ethical Management.* New York: Morrow.

Boisot, M. (1995) "Preparing for Turbulence: The Changing Relationship Between Strategy and Management Development in the Learning Organization," *Developing Strategic Thought: Rediscovering the Art of Direction-Giving.* London: McGraw-Hill.

Branson, R.K. (1988: April) "Why Schools Can't Improve: The Upper Limit Hypothesis," *The Journal of Instructional Development.*

Braswell, P.C., Sims, L., & Kaufman, R. (1994: August) *A Report on Return on Investment of Vocational Occupational Preparatory Particpants.* Tallahassee, FL: The Center for Needs Assessment & Planning, The Learning Systems Institute, Florida State University.

Dick, W., & Johnson, F.C. (Eds.) "Special Issue on Quality Systems in *Performance Improvement.*" *Performance Improvement Quarterly*, Vol. 6, No. 3.

Dow Chemical (1991: April) "Our Quality Coaches," *Technical Assistance Methodology* (Supplement Issue).

Fink, R. (1993: September) "Group Therapy: That's Benchmarking," *Financial World.*

Garratt, B. (1987) *The Learning Organization.* London: HarperCollins.

Gilbert, T.F. (1978) *Human Competence: Engineering Worthy Performance.* New York: McGraw-Hill Book Co.

Gilbert, T.F., & Gilbert, M.B. (1989: January) "Performance Engineering: Making Human Productiviey a Science," *Performance & Instruction.*

Hammer, M., & Champy, J. (1993) *Reengineering the Corporation: A Manifesto for Business Revolution.* New York: Harper Business.

Hanford, P. (1995) "Developing Director and Executive Competencies in Strategic Thinking," *Developing Strategic Thought: Rediscovering the Art of Direction-Giving.* London: McGraw-Hill.

Harless, J.H. (1975) *An Ounce of Analysis Is Worth a Pound of Cure.* Newnan, GA: Harless Performance Guild.

Hinchliffe, D.R. (1990: September) "Implications for Using Outcome/Mega Planning Referents in Military Training." *Performance & Instruction.*

Hinchliffe, D.R. (1995) *Training for Results: Determining Education and Training Needs for Emergency Management in Australia* (unpublished doctoral dissertation). Monash University, Clayton Campus, Victoria, Australia.

Kanter, R.M. (1989) *When Giants Learn to Dance: Mastering the Challenges of Strategy, Management, and Careers in the 1990s.* New York: Simon & Schuster.

Kaufman, R., & Carron, A.S. (1980: April) "Utility and Self-Sufficiency in the Selection of Educational Alternatives." *Journal of Instructional Development*, pp. 14–18, 23–26.

Kaufman, R., Grise, P., & Watters, K. (1992) "Deriving a Vision," In K.L. Medsker and D.G. Roberts (Eds.), *ASTD Trainer's Toolkit: Evaluating the Results of Training*, p. 86. Alexandria, VA: The American Society for Training & Development.

Kaufman, R., Gavora, M., & James, A. (1993: July) *Healthy Start Evaluation: A Study to Cooperatively Develop a Practical Evaluation Framework and Define Useful Evaluation Criteria*. Tallahassee, FL: The Center for Needs Assessment & Planning, The Learning Systems Institute, Florida State University.

Levin, H.M. (1983) *Cost Effectiveness: A Primer (New Perspectives in Evaluation)*. Beverly Hills, CA: Sage .

MacGillis, P., Hintzen, N., & Kaufman, R. (1989) "Problems and Prospects of Implementing a Holistic Planning Framework in Vocational Education: Applications of the Organizational Elements Model," *Performance Improvement Quarterly*, Vol. 2, No. 1.

Mager, R.F., & Pipe, P. (1983) *CRI: Criterion Referenced Instruction* (2nd Ed.). Carefree, AZ: Mager Associates.

Murphy, B., & Swanson, R., (1988) "Auditing Training and Development," *Journal of European Industrial Training*.

Roberts, W. (1987) *Leadership Secrets of Attila the Hun*. New York: Warner.

Stolovitch, H.D., & Keeps, E.J. (1992) *Handbook of Human Performance Technology: A Comprehensive Guide for Analyzing and Solving Performance Problems in Organizations*. San Francisco: Jossey-Bass.

Wilkinson, D. (1989) "Outputs and Outcomes of Vocational Educatioanl Programs: Measures in Australia," *Performance Improvement Quarterly*, Vol. 2, No. 2.

Xerox Corporation. (1989) *Leadership Through Quality Processes and Tools Review: Quality You Can Copy*. Rochester, NY: Multinational Customer & Service Education.

About the Author

Roger Kaufman is professor and director of the Center for Needs Assessment and Planning at Florida State University. He is also research professor of engineering management at the Newark College of Engineering of the New Jersey Institute of Technology and is associated with the faculty of Industrial Engineering Systems at the University of Central Florida. He has been a professor at the United States International University and Chapman University, and has taught at the University of Southern California and at Pepperdine University. He was the 1983 Haydn Williams Fellow at the Curtin University of Technology in Perth, Australia. His PhD in communications is from New York University, with graduate work in industrial engineering, psychology, and education at the University of California at Berkeley and at Johns Hopkins University. Before entering higher education, Kaufman was assistant to the vice-president for research and to the vice-president for engineering at Douglas Aircraft Company; before that, he was director of training system analysis at US Industries, head of human factors engineering at Martin Baltimore, and human factors specialist at Boeing. He served two terms on the US secretary of the Navy's Advisory Board on Education and Training.

Among Kaufman's past and current clients, in the areas of strategic planning, quality management, needs assessment, and organizational improvement, are Andersen Consulting, Chase Manhattan Bank, Los Alamos National Laboratories, AT&T, The World Bank, the Florida Department of Education, the National Academy of School Executives, the American Society for Curriculum and Development, Parke-Davis, McDonnell-Douglas, the New Zealand Department of Health, and many others. He is a fellow of the American Psychological Association and of the American Academy of School Psychology, and is a diplomate of the American Board of Professional Psychology. He has published 30 books and more than 155 articles on strategic planning, quality management and continuous improvement, needs assessment, management, and evaluation.

About the Publishers

Founded in 1944, the American Society for Training and Development (ASTD) is the world's premier professional association in the field of workplace learning and performance. ASTD's membership includes more than 58,000 people in organizations from every level of the field of workplace performance in more than 100 countries. Its leadership and members work in more than 15,000 multinational corporations, small and medium-sized businesses, government agencies, colleges, and universities. ASTD is the leading resource on workplace learning and performance issues, providing information, research, analysis, and practical information derived from its own research, the knowledge and experience of its members, its conferences and publications, and the coalitions and partnerships it has built through research and policy work. For more information on ASTD products, services, or membership, please call 703/683-8100 or fax 703/683-1523.

Founded in 1962, the International Society for Performance Improvement (ISPI) is the leading international association dedicated to improving productivity and performance in the workplace. ISPI represents more than 10,000 international and chapter members throughout the United States, Canada, and 33 other countries. ISPI's mission is to improve the performance of individuals and organizations through the application of human performance technology. Assembling an Annual Conference & Expo and other educational events, publishing several periodicals, and producing publications like *Strategic Thinking* are some of the ways ISPI works toward achieving this mission. For more information, please write ISPI, 1300 L Street, NW, Suite 1250, Washington, DC 20005.